how2become

Royal Marines Officer

The ULTIMATE guide for anyone who is serious about passing the selection process for becoming an Elite Royal Marines Officer

www.How2Become.com

As part of this product you have also received FREE access to online tests that will help you to pass the Royal Marines selection process

To gain access, simply go to:

www.MyPsychometricTests.co.uk

Get more products for passing any test at:

www.How2Become.com

Orders: Please contact How2Become Ltd, Suite 14, 50 Churchill Square Business Centre, Kings Hill, Kent ME19 4YU.

You can order through Amazon.co.uk under ISBN: **9781907558719**, via the website www.How2Become.com or through Gardners.com.

ISBN: **9781907558719**

First published in 2011 by How2Become Ltd.

Updated in 2018.

Typeset by Katie Noakes for How2Become Ltd.

Disclaimer

Every effort has been made to ensure that the information contained within this guide is accurate at the time of publication. How2Become Ltd is not responsible for anyone failing any part of any selection process as a result of the information contained within this guide. How2Become Ltd and their authors cannot accept any responsibility for any errors or omissions within this guide, however caused. No responsibility for loss or damage occasioned by any person acting, or refraining from action, as a result of the material in this publication can be accepted by How2Become Ltd.

The information within this guide does not represent the views of any third party service or organisation.

CONTENTS

Welcome

Welcome to your new guide – How to pass the Royal Marines Officer selection process. This guide has been designed to help you prepare for, and pass, the Royal Marines Officer selection process, including the Admiralty Interview Board (AIB) and the Potential Officer's Course (POC).

The author of this guide, Richard McMunn, has spent over 20 years in both the Royal Navy and the Emergency Services. He has vast experience and knowledge in the area of Armed Forces recruitment and you will find his guidance both inspiring and highly informative. During his successful career in the Fire Service, Richard sat on many interview panels assessing candidates applying for positions within the Fire Service. He has also been extremely successful at passing job interviews and assessments himself and has a success rate of over 90%. Follow his advice and preparation techniques carefully and you too can achieve the same levels of success in your career.

Whilst the selection process for joining the Royal Marines as an Officer is highly competitive, there are a number of things you can do in order to improve your chances of success, and they are all contained within this guide.

The guide itself has been split up into useful sections to make it easier for you to prepare for each stage. Read each section carefully and take notes as you progress. Don't ever give up on your dreams; if you really want to become an elite Royal Marines Officer, then you can do it! The way to prepare for a job in the Armed Forces as an Officer is to embark on a programme of 'in depth' preparation, and this guide will show you exactly how to do just that!

If you need any further help with the Royal Marines Officer aptitude tests, Planning Exercises, getting fit, or RM Officer Interview advice, then we offer a wide range of products to assist you.

These are all available through our website:

www.How2Become.com

Once again thank you for your custom and we wish you every success in your pursuit to joining the Royal Marines as an Officer.

Work hard, stay focused, and secure your dream career!

Best wishes,

The how2become team

The How2Become Team

Preface By Richard McMunn

I can remember sitting in the Armed Forces careers office in Preston, Lancashire at the age of 16 waiting patiently to see the Warrant Officer who would interview me as part of my application for joining the Royal Navy. I had already passed the written tests, and despite never having sat an interview before in my life, I was confident of success.

In the build up to the interview, I had worked very hard studying the job that I was applying for, and also working hard on my interview technique. At the end of the interview I was told that I had easily passed and all that was left to complete was the medical. Unfortunately, I was overweight at the time and I was worried that I might fail. At the medical my fears became a reality and I was told by the doctor that I would have to lose a stone in weight before they would accept me. I walked out of the doctor's surgery and began to walk to the bus stop that would take me back home three miles away. I was absolutely gutted, and embarrassed, that I had failed at the final hurdle, all because I was overweight!

I sat at the bus stop feeling sorry for myself and wondering what job I was going to apply for next. My dream of joining the Armed Forces was over and I didn't know which way to turn. Suddenly, I began to feel a sense of determination to lose the weight and get fit in the shortest time possible. It was at that particular point in my life when things would change forever. As the bus approached I remember thinking there was no time like the present for getting started on my fitness regime. I therefore opted to walk the three miles home instead of being lazy and getting the bus. When I got home I sat in my room and wrote out a 'plan of action' that would dictate how I was going to lose the weight required. That plan of action was very simple and contained the following three rules:

1. Every weekday morning I will get up at 6am and run 3 miles.
2. Instead of catching the bus to college and then back home again, I will walk.
3. I will eat healthily and I will not go over the recommended daily calorific intake.

Every day I would read my simple 'action plan' and it acted as a reminder of what I needed to do. Within a few weeks of following my plan rigidly, I had lost over a stone in weight and I was a lot fitter too!

When I returned back to the doctor's surgery for my medical the doctor was amazed that I had managed to lose the weight in such a short space of time and he was pleased that I had been so determined to pass the medical. Six months later I started my basic training course with the Royal Navy.

Ever since then I have always made sure that I prepare properly for any job application. If I do fail a particular interview or section of an application process, then I will always go out of my way to ask for feedback so that I can improve for next time. I also still use an 'action plan' in just about every element of my work. Action plans allow you to focus your mind on what you want to achieve and I will be teaching you how to use them to great effect during this guide.

Throughout my career I have always been successful. It's not because I am better than the next person, but simply because I prepare better. I didn't do very well at school so I have to work a lot harder to pass the exams and written tests that form part of a job application process, but I am always aware of what I need to do and what I must improve on.

I have always been a great believer in preparation. Preparation was my key to success, and it will also be yours. Without the right level of preparation you will be setting out on the route to failure. The Royal Marines are difficult to join, but if you follow the steps that I have compiled within this guide, then you will increase your chances of success.

Remember, you are learning how to be a successful candidate, not a successful marine – that will come later!

The men and women of the Armed Forces carry out an amazing job. They are there to protect us and our country and they do that job with great pride, passion and very high levels of professionalism and commitment. They are to be congratulated for the job that they do.

Before you apply to join the Royal Marines you need to be fully confident that you too are capable of providing that same level of commitment. If you think you can do it, and you can rise to the challenge, then you just might be the type of person the Royal Marines are looking for.

As you progress through this guide, you will notice that the qualities required to join the Royal Marines are a common theme. You must learn these qualities, and also be able to demonstrate throughout the selection process that you can meet them, if you are to have any chance of successfully passing the selection process.

Best wishes,

Richard McMunn

Chapter 1
The Commando State of Mind

You are not applying to join the Royal Marines as a Commando, but it is still important that you understand the values and the ethos that each man is required to follow. After all, if you do not know the values and the ethos, how can you be expected to implement them as an Officer and leader?

In addition to this, as an Officer you too must demonstrate the correct state of mind. Before I even begin to talk about the Royal Marines Officer selection process, you must learn how important it is to adopt the correct state of mind. If you have it, then you are far more likely to succeed and pass the selection process.

Picture the scene, you are at the Potential Officers Course (POC) and you are taking part in the Endurance Course. You are totally shattered and your body wants to stop. You've simply had enough and you're not sure that your body can take any more. The majority of other candidates have already stopped and you are desperate to give in. What do you do?

The problem with this kind of scenario is that it is new to you. Not many of us find ourselves in these kinds of situations ever in our lifetime. Therefore our minds are not tuned to cope with it, and the natural reaction is to quit.

Your muscles are telling your mind that they can't take any more and they send a signal to your brain basically saying enough is enough! It's at this point that you're going to be different. This is the difference between your average person and a RM Officer. Regardless of how much you ache, or regardless of how much your body is telling you to quit, your mind will be telling you something completely different. To put it simply, you never give in, even if your body can't move any further along that Endurance Course, you just don't give in.

During my career I've been in this type of situation on numerous occasions. Some of them have been life or death situations. One in particular was whilst serving as a firefighter on White Watch at Maidstone Fire Station. It was approximately 1745 hours on a cold winter's afternoon and I was due to go off shift at 1800 hours. It was a Friday and I was looking forward to going out on the town with my mates. All of a sudden, the bells went down and we were turned out to a fire in a furniture store located in the town centre.

When we arrived, black smoke was billowing out of the front entrance door and windows, and a rather stressful shop owner was urging us to get a move on. As you can imagine, his shop was in serious danger of burning to the ground. I'd not long been out of my recruit training and I had not experienced that many 'severe' fires yet. It was my turn to wear breathing apparatus so I quickly got rigged up, went under air, and then followed the senior firefighter into the building. What was about to happen was one of the most frightening experiences I have ever encountered in my life. I was about to be tested to the limit.

As we entered the building I could sense something wasn't quite right. The smoke was becoming thicker and blacker by the second and the temperature was rising quickly. The signs of flashover and backdraught were relatively new to the fire service at the time, so we weren't fully aware of the dangerous situation we were entering into. We made our way up to the third floor quickly, taking a hose with us so that we could tackle the fire, and also retrace our steps on the way out. We had been told that the fire was probably in a room on the upper floors of the building, so we started to search for the fire in line with our training and procedures.

After approximately ten minutes the heat inside the building became unbearable, and I couldn't see my hand in front of my face due to the thick, black acrid smoke. I concentrated on my training, took deep breaths and checked my air regularly. I was very fit at the time and hadn't used that much air from my cylinder. My colleague shouted in my ear that he couldn't see the fire anywhere and that maybe we should start thinking about evacuating the building due to the intensity of the heat. I think his words were something more along the lines of "let's get the f**k out of here, the heat's starting to burn my shoulders!"

Just as we started to retrace our steps we heard a noise that was every firefighter's worst nightmare. Outside, the fire had become so intense that the officer-in-charge had decided it was time to get us out. Basically, he had initiated the evacuation procedure, which consisted of short blasts of an acme thunderer whistle. All we could hear from inside the building was whistles being blown – we knew we were in trouble. Even though it was a long time ago now, the thought of it still makes the hairs stand up on the back of my neck. I'd heard of incidents where firefighters had lost their lives in building fires, and I thought that it now might be my turn.

We quickly started to retrace our steps, following the hose carefully. I'd started to become slightly disorientated due to the heat, but I knew the hose reel would guide us back down the stairs and to ultimate safety. How wrong could I be! As we approached the top of the stairs the hose suddenly disappeared. My colleague turned to me and shouted that the hose had become trapped under some fallen furniture and that he couldn't find the other end of it – we were now in serious trouble. The hose was basically our lifeline, which would lead us to safety, and now we didn't have it. We sat together and took deep breaths. The whistles were still blaring outside and we knew that the only way to get out of this building was to try as hard as possible to conserve our air and remain calm. All I could think about was my girlfriend and how much I wanted to see her again. That thought in my mind gave me the confidence and determination to push on and get out of the building to safety.

We decided to locate a wall, and then simply follow it in the direction that our instincts told us would lead to the top of the stairs. We eventually came to the top of some stairs, but there was a problem. We could not locate the hose, which effectively meant that this flight of stairs was not the flight we had used to gain access to the building in the first place. Basically we had no choice, we had to go down them and just hope that they led us outside. As we progressed down the stairs my heart was beating like never before.
I remember thinking that these stairs could be leading us to a cellar or basement area and that we would become trapped.

Thankfully, as we made our way down the stairs we heard voices. The officer-in-charge had sent in an emergency crew to help locate us. We met them halfway down the stairs and they then led us out to safety. I can remember making my way outside of the building and looking back at the store, which had already been half demolished by the inferno. Another few minutes in there and I would have been dead, that's for sure. As I took off my breathing apparatus set, which was caked in soot, the officer-in-charge looked over at me with a huge sign of relief on his face. If only he knew how I was feeling!

I learnt a tremendous amount from that incident. The first thing I learnt was how important it is to remain calm in every crisis situation. Even when things are really bad, the only way that you'll achieve a successful outcome is by staying calm and focused. The second thing I learnt from that experience was the importance of comradeship and teamwork. The fire service is very similar to the Royal Marines in the fact that everyone looks out for each other. Everyone in the team is dependent on each other. You do your job properly and the team will be just fine. Break the rules, be unprofessional or disorganised, and things will go wrong, it's as simple as that!

The Commando state of mind involves the following key areas:
- Confidence;
- Strength;
- Independence;
- Ability.

Each one of the above qualities is exceptional in an individual. If you have them all, then you are a serious contender for becoming a Royal Marines Commando. Of course, it will be slightly different for you. You are applying to become an Officer and therefore you will require an additional set of attributes; more on these later.

Now I'm not saying that you need to have all of these qualities polished off before you apply to become a Royal Marines Officer, but a knowledge of how important they are and also how to demonstrate them in certain situations will go a long way to helping you succeed. Let's now take a look at each of them individually.

CONFIDENCE
Confidence is at the top of the list for me personally when it comes to achieving what I want in life. There is a vast difference, however, between confidence and arrogance. I am confident because I believe in my own abilities. I work hard to improve on my weak areas and I also believe in those people around me. I am not afraid to take risks that I believe are worth taking, and I am certainly not afraid to put my own life at risk to save others.

As a Royal Marines Officer you will need confidence in abundance. You should never ask a commando to do something that you would not be prepared to do yourself. As the saying goes…lead by example.

Whilst going through selection demonstrate a high level of confidence, but never cross the line into arrogance. The selection staff want to see that you have the guts to keep running when you're absolutely shattered, and when your body is telling you to stop. They want to see that that you have the confidence to put yourself forward, when others around you stand back.

During the Potential Officer's Course you will be required to undertake a confidence test. During day 2 of the POC you will receive a demonstration of the "Commando slide" and "punch into the net" obstacles of the "Tarzan Assault Course". You will then be expected to complete both obstacles, during which the POC staff will assess your confidence to operate effectively at heights.

Confidence comes with time and with experience, but there is no reason why you can't start improving it right now in preparation for selection.

STRENGTH

To the majority of people, the word 'strength' means the ability to lift heavy weights or objects. To the Commando, it is not just about physical strength, but also about strength of the mind. The only obstacle in your way to passing officer selection is your own mind. Fill it with doubt and negative thoughts, and the end result is virtually guaranteed to be failure. Yes, of course you must work on your physical strength and fitness, but if your mind isn't tuned into what you want to achieve, then you are going nowhere.

Allow me to give you an example of where strength of mind can work to your advantage. Whilst going through the selection process for becoming a firefighter, I was required to attend an intense physical assessment day. Amongst other things, the assessment involved a requirement to:

- Bench press 50kg, 20 times within 60 seconds;
- Run around a field for an hour whilst carrying a heavy object between a small group;
- A claustrophobia test involving crawling through sewer pipes in the dark whilst wearing a blacked out mask;

- Assembling items of equipment;
- Knots and lines;
- Hose running.

The hose running assessment was carried out at the end of the day. Out of twenty people who had started the day, there were just six of us left. Although I was exhausted, there was absolutely no way I was going to fail the hose running assessment. This assessment had a reputation for being gruelling. It entailed running out lengths of heavy 25 metre hose whilst wearing full firefighting uniform, and then making it back up again in a prescribed manner. It sounds like a simple task, but coupled with the sheer exhaustion that was already taking its toll on my body, and the fact that I was wearing an ill-fitting firefighter's uniform, this was no easy task.

The Station Officer started off by making us do ten runs, just to warm up. Whilst we were carrying out the runs, a Sub Officer would walk next to us shouting in our ears how 'useless' he thought we were, and that he knew 'how much we wanted to give in.' I won't tell you what else he said but you get the drift!

After the first ten runs we were then required to do a further 25 in succession. Soon after we started, two men dropped out, leaving just the four of us remaining. We all managed to complete the 25 runs although I was ready to crumble and I know for certain that I couldn't have done any more.

We all stood there in a line with our hoses made up, ready for the next set of instructions. The Station Officer walked up and down with his stick and clipboard, making us wait in anticipation – he was clearly loving every minute of it! My legs were shaking and I could feel my heart pounding so fast it felt like it was about to jump out of my skin.

Then, the Station Officer spoke once more – "OK, pick up your hoses and get ready for another 25 runs!" 25 more runs I thought! You must be joking!

At that point I was at a crossroads in my life. Give in now and all that hard work training to pass the firefighter selection would be out of the window. But if I try to press on, then there's absolutely no way I can manage another 25 runs!

It was at that point that a thought came into my mind. Whether I could do the next set of 25 runs or not was irrelevant. What was important was that I carried on and I didn't give in. So I did. I picked up my hose and waited for the Station Officer to tell us to commence. He then turned round and said – "Well done guys, you've passed. Put the hoses down and grab yourselves a glass of water." I couldn't believe it; he was just testing us to see if we had the strength of mind to continue, even though our bodies couldn't take anymore – a valuable lesson in determination and strength of mind if ever I saw one.

Mindset is extremely important whilst preparing for selection. You will need to be organised and disciplined and you will need to concentrate on improving your weak areas. Remember that the quality of strength is not just about lifting or carrying heavy objects, but the strength of your mind also.

INDEPENDENCE
The quality of independence is all about being able to look after yourself and being capable of carrying out your role within the team to a professional standard. Once a Commando has completed the rigorous training course, he will be expected to look after himself, his kit and his life in general. Yes there will be continuous training exercises and development sessions, but the overall maintenance of the kit, weapons and physical fitness is down to each individual. The same rule applies to you as an Officer. Neglect any of these important elements and you will be letting yourself and the team down.

Royal Marines depend on each other. You will depend on your colleagues within the Corp to carry out their job to a high standard, and they will depend on you also.

ABILITY
Ability is the quality of being able to do something, especially the physical and mental power to accomplish something.

Not everyone has the ability to become a Royal Marines Commando or a Royal Marines Officer. That's one of the reasons why the Corp have used the strap line '99.9% need not apply' during past recruitment campaigns. It wasn't designed to put people off, but more importantly designed to make people aware that you need a large amount of 'ability', not only to pass the selection process, but also to become a competent Marine. If you have the ability, then you can be trained.

The Commando State of Mind should not only be something that you learn, but it should also be something that you strive to demonstrate during selection. You will also have the added responsibility of ensuring that the men under your command stick to it!

Have the confidence in your own abilities, have the strength of mind to achieve and persevere; be independent and also have the ability to learn new things and accomplish your goals.

TOP TIPS ON HOW TO PREPARE FOR, AND PASS THE ROYAL MARINES OFFICER SELECTION PROCESS

TIP 1 – THE RIGHT MENTAL APPROACH

Without the correct mental approach your chances of passing selection will be limited. There is a tremendous amount of pressure on you during both selection and during the build-up. Not only do you have to improve your fitness, you also have to work on your leadership ability, your teamwork ability, your speed, distance and time competence and also your interview skills and psychometric testing ability. It is crucial that you are organised. It is crucial that you prepare thoroughly and it is also crucial that your mind-set is one of 'can do' attitude.

This means getting up early every morning and making sure you can easily pass all of the minimum standards expected during selection; including the AIB and the POC. It is also about having the mind-set that you will not give in, despite what your body will be telling you. There will be times during selection when you've simply had enough. These are the times when you must push yourself forward and keep going despite the fatigue and the physical agony. There will also be times during selection when you will need to remain calm whilst working under pressure. This will particularly be the case during the planning exercise element of the Admiralty Interview Board, more on this later.

TIP 2 – USE AN ACTION PLAN TO ENSURE SUCCESS

Action plans are a great way to measure your progress during pre-selection preparation. I use an action plan in just about everything I do that is work-related. An action plan basically sets out what you intend to do, and when you intend to do it. An example of a very basic action plan that is focused on fitness preparation might look like this:

- MONDAY – 6am start, run 3 miles (best effort), record my time.
- TUESDAY – 6 am start, 50 press-ups, 50 sit-ups, making sure I concentrate on the correct technique.
- WEDNESDAY – 10-mile run, then 50 sit-ups and 50 press-ups, making sure I concentrate on the correct technique.
- THURSDAY – Swim 25 lengths of my local swimming pool (breaststroke).
- FRIDAY – 6am start, 10 pull-ups, 50 press-ups and 50 sit-ups, making sure I concentrate on the correct technique.
- SATURDAY – Rest day.
- SUNDAY – 5-mile brisk walk.

During the following week you may decide to increase the intensity of your workouts and the number of repetitions that you are performing.

The point I am trying to make here is that if you use an action plan, you are far more likely to make significant progress. If you stick the action plan in a prominent position at home, such as the fridge door, then it will act as a reminder of what you need to do the following day.

Here is a list of just a few areas you may wish to include on your action plan:
- Improving your fitness;
- Your knowledge of current affairs;
- Psychometric test questions practice;
- Interview preparation;
- Speed, distance and time test sessions;
- Knowledge of the Royal Marines and the Royal Navy;
- Military equipment, personnel, bases and staff.

TIP 3 – DON'T NEGLECT YOUR APTITUDE/PSYCHOMETRIC TESTING ABILITY

Whilst I recommend that you spend the majority of your pre-selection preparation working hard on your fitness, you should not neglect the important area of aptitude/psychometric testing. During the selection process you will be required to pass a series of tests. The tests will form part of the Admiralty Interview Board and will consist of:

- a 20-minute verbal reasoning test designed to demonstrate your general reasoning and ability with words.
- a 13-minute non-verbal reasoning test, again measuring your reasoning power, but this time without the emphasis on verbal skills.
- a 25-minute numerical test covering numerical fluency, reasoning and statistics.
- a 15-minute speed and accuracy test, measuring your concentration and mental agility.
- a 15-minute spatial orientation test, involving directions, relative positions and movement.
- a short general service knowledge test to provide the Board with an indication of your research into the Royal Navy.

I recommend that you spend at least 30 minutes every evening of the week working on your ability to pass these tests. You can obtain free sample psychometric test questions to help you prepare for these tests at the following link:

www.MyPsychometricTests.co.uk

In addition to becoming competent in the use of psychometric tests you will also need to be highly proficient in the use of speed, distance and time. I have dedicated an entire section of this guide to this important testing area; however, you can also obtain online test questions at the following website:

www.speeddistancetime.info

TIP 4 – TRAIN HARD, RACE EASY
If somebody finds a test or assessment easy, it generally means that they have prepared hard for it. If you work hard in the weeks leading up to the POC and AIB, then your chances of success will greatly increase. Yes, you will find it tough, but if you've trained well above the minimum standards that are required, then you can pass with flying colours.

When I was 26 I decided to carry out an Iron Man challenge for a local charity. This involved swimming 2 miles, then running a marathon, before finishing off with a 120-mile cycle ride. I managed to achieve all of this within 9 hours. Whilst it was mentally tough, the physical aspect was easy.

It was easy because I'd trained extremely hard in the 6 months leading up to the challenge. Train hard in the build up to selection, and you will certainly race easy!

TIP 5 – BLEEP TEST PREPARATION

Lots of people neglect to try out the bleep test before they go through selection. During the POC you will be required to reach level 11, so make sure you can easily achieve this before you go. There are no excuses for not getting yourself a copy of the test and practising it. You can obtain a copy of the test at:

www.How2Become.com.

Alternatively, you can download a copy of the test and get yourself lots of tips and advice on how to prepare for Royal Marines selection, at the following website:

www.royalmarinestraining.co.uk

TIP 6 – TECHNIQUE IS CRUCIAL

During the POC you will be required to carry out a number of sit-ups, press-ups and pull-ups, within a two-minute period. Being able to reach the minimum standard is only part of it; you must also perform them using the correct technique. During the build up to selection, make sure you practice each of the above utilising the correct technique. I will explain the correct technique during the POC section of the guide. This will not only make your life a lot easier during the POC, but it will also impress the instructors and show them that you have really gone out of your way to meet their requirements.

TIP 7 – YOU ARE WHAT YOU EAT (AND DRINK)

Let's face it; a diet of lager, burgers, chips and kebabs isn't going to help you get the most out of your training sessions. In the build-up to officer selection fill yourself with the right types of foods and also make sure you drink plenty of water. You will need the water to keep yourself hydrated.

Foods such as fish, chicken, vegetables, fruit, rice and potatoes are all rich in the right types of nutrients, which will allow you to perform to the best of your ability. Try to cut out caffeine, alcohol and all forms of takeaway food in the build-up to selection. You will feel a lot better for it and you will be able to work harder for longer.

TIP 8 – PRACTICE A MOCK INTERVIEW

Before you attend the AFCO interview, and even the POC and AIB, try out a mock interview at home. A mock interview basically involves getting a friend or relative to sit down and ask you all of the interview questions that are contained within this guide. This will give you the opportunity to practice your responses to the questions before you do the real thing. The Royal Marines selecting officers are looking for people who are confident in their own abilities.

During the interview you will want to portray a level of confidence and you can achieve this by working through your answers before you attend the real thing.

I also recommend that you work on your interview technique. This involves:
- Walking into the interview room looking smart and well presented. Stand tall and do not slouch.
- Don't sit down in the interview chair until invited to do so.
- Be respectful and courteous towards the interview panel. Address them as 'sir' unless told otherwise.
- Maintain eye contact during the interview, but don't stare them out!
- Never slouch in the interview chair. Sit upright at all times and do not fidget.
- When responding to the interview questions avoid any form of waffle. They will see right through it. Be honest in your responses at all times.

TIP 9 – BE COMPETENT IN THE USE OF SPEED, DISTANCE AND TIME

I cannot stress enough how important it is to be fully competent in the use of speed, distance and time. You must ensure that you can carry out calculations in SDT quickly, both in writing and in your head, without the aid of pen and paper.

You will be placed under considerable pressure during the planning exercise stage of the Admiralty Interview Board; one of the final stages of selection. During a later stage of this guide, I have provided you with a section dedicated to SDT.

TIP 10 – BE FULLY UP-TO-DATE WITH CURRENT AFFAIRS

There is a saying that goes 'you are what you eat.' When it comes to Royal Marines Officer selection you could also say that 'you are what you read.'

I strongly advise that you spend plenty of time reading good quality newspapers in the build up to selection. Personally, I would start reading the Times. I would also subscribe to The Week magazine and The Economist. These are fantastic ways to improve both your diction and your current affair knowledge. I will explain more about current affairs later on in this guide.

Chapter 2
The Selection Process

The majority of people who will read this guide will have a thorough understanding of what the Royal Marines Officer selection process consists of. Before I get into each element of selection however, and more importantly how to pass them, it is important for me to briefly explain the different elements.

To begin with, applicants will need to contact their local Armed Forces Careers Office and explain that they wish to apply to become an Officer with the Royal Marines. The Royal Marines form part of the Royal Navy so it is highly likely that your first port of call (excuse the pun) will be with the RN careers advisor.

The most effective way to do this is to go along to your nearest centre for a brief chat. You will be supplied with an information pack and details on how to apply, providing you meet the minimum eligibility requirements.

THE FILTER INTERVIEW
You will eventually be invited to attend what is called a 'filter' interview. This interview is designed to assess whether or not you have the right qualities to become a Royal Marines Officer. If you successfully pass the filter interview, which is usually held at the Armed Forces Careers Office, you will be recommended to attend the Potential Officers Course (POC). If you pass the POC, then you will go to the Admiralty Interview Board (AIB). The filter interview is, in my opinion, relatively easy to pass. However, you will still need to put in plenty of preparation and I have provided you with a host of sample questions and responses during a later section of this guide.

THE POTENTIAL OFFICERS COURSE
The POC is designed to see whether you are likely to meet the challenge of being a Royal Marines Officer. As the title suggests, it is a test of your potential so you must prepare fully and give it your all if you are to have any chance of succeeding.

It is an immensely gruelling test of your physical fitness, and above all looks at your determination and commitment. In addition to the above, you must also demonstrate leadership potential, intelligence, how you communicate, and whether you can keep a sense of humour even when you are absolutely exhausted.

The POC also gives you the opportunity to find out more about the Royal Marines. Many candidates find out during the POC that it simply isn't for them and decide not to carry on with selection. It is also a unique chance to learn a lot about yourself and your strengths and weaknesses. The POC takes place at the Commando Training Centre Royal Marines (CTCRM), Lympstone, Devon. The base is situated on the banks of the Exe estuary, 8 miles south-east of Exeter. Courses run approximately twice a month throughout the year increasing in frequency between March and July. The POC lasts for 52 hours spread over 3 days from 0900 Monday to lunchtime Wednesday.

BEFORE YOU ARRIVE
You will receive comprehensive joining instructions 3-4 weeks prior to the course providing all administrative details and a rail warrant if you requested one.

If you want to give your best on the POC, thorough preparation is vital.

DAY ONE
0800 – ARRIVAL
You are required to arrive at CTCRM no later than 0800 on Monday. Candidates are advised to turn up on the Sunday if travelling some distance but regardless of the distance you are travelling we strongly recommend you arrive the night before. Take this initial opportunity to get to know other members of the course, since you will need to work as a team over the next 48 hours. Passing the POC is about meeting a standard – the standard demanded of a potential Royal Marines Officer – not competing with others. You will be met by the Course Supervisor in the Mess at 0900 for an informal brief prior to the course commencing. Once you have been briefed by the Course Supervisor you will be issued with kit and then have your course photograph taken. This is followed by a presentation from the Course Officer detailing the content of the POC which you will experience over the following 2 days.

1145 – ROYAL MARINES FITNESS ASSESSMENT (RMFA)
You will move to the gymnasium to undertake the Royal Marines

Fitness Assessment (RMFA). To begin with, the Physical Training Staff will brief you on the way you will be expected to conduct yourself during the RMFA. You will then begin the assessment, which consists of the following.

(IMPORTANT: READ THE EXERCISE TECHNIQUES DETAILED ON THE FOLLOWING PAGES)

- **2.4 KILOMETRE RUN**

You will be expected to complete a 2.4 kilometre run on astroturf. If you do not meet the requirements based on age and gender, you will not be able to proceed to the next stage of selection.

- **PRESS-UP TEST**

The duration of the test is 2 minutes, 60 press-ups will get you maximum points. The body must be kept straight at all times, the chest will be lowered to meet another student's fist, you must then fully lock out the arms on the upward motion. Your hands will be shoulder width apart and your elbows must be kept into your side, poor form will result in you being stopped.

- **SIT-UP TEST**

Once again the test will last for 2 minutes, 85 repetitions will get you maximum points. Your feet will be held by a partner, your fingers must stay in contact with your temples and your elbows must make contact with the mat on the rearward motion and come up to touch the knees on the upward motion, your knees must be kept together, poor form will result in you being stopped.

- **PULL-UP TEST**

This exercise will be carried out on the wooden beam. You will adopt an "overhand grasp", your body will hang straight and then be pulled up until your chin is over the beam. The exercise will be done to the commands of "bend and stretch" this is to ensure strictness and prevent the use of momentum, you will be told to "drop off" if you do not stay in time. To gain maximum points you must achieve 16 repetitions.

All 4 RMFA tests have a maximum score of 100 points each. The overall RMFA pass mark is 180 out of 400 points (160 for RM Scholars).

Any candidate scoring below 180 points on the overall RMFA will be withdrawn from the course.

1400 – WEAPONS PRESENTATION

You will be taken for a Specialist Weapons brief by a member of the POC team, you will also get a chance to have a 'hands on' with some of the weapons displayed.

1530 – ESSAY AND INTERVIEW

Next, the emphasis changes from physical to mental prowess, as you will write a short essay on a current affairs topic. You will be given a choice of at least two subjects, a time limit of 1 hour and a maximum of 2 sides of A4. What we are looking for – apart from accurate grammar and spelling – is your ability to reason, justify your arguments and communicate clearly on paper. Your knowledge of current defence related issues is important.

During the essay the Course Officer or Assisting Officer will take each candidate aside for a short individual interview. This will help them get to know you, assess your level of Corps knowledge and to find out why you want to join the Royal Marines as an Officer.

DAY TWO

0720 – CONFIDENCE TESTS & BOTTOM FIELD SESSION

After breakfast, you will be met by the Course Supervisor and taken for a thorough warm-up prior to beginning the morning's physical activities. You will then receive a demonstration of the "Commando slide" and "punch into the net" obstacles of the "Tarzan Assault Course".

The candidates will then be expected to complete both obstacles, allowing the POC staff to gauge candidates' confidence to operate effectively at heights. The candidates will then be led to the bottom field where they will receive a demonstration of how to tackle each obstacle on the Assault Course. On completion of the demonstration it will be your turn to do a 'timed run'.

Then you will be split into teams for the log race, where each team has to carry a log around the course without it touching the ground. For some of the obstacles, you will be the team leader, for others a team member – and on other obstacles there will be no leader designated. First you will have a short time in which to work out how you are going to tackle each obstacle. You will then have to brief your team clearly and positively before putting your plan into action. It will test your drive and assertiveness, how well you communicate under pressure, and how well you work as a team member when someone else is leading.

Next you will undertake 2 Fireman's carries – 200m in under 90 seconds and 100m in under 45 seconds. You will then get cleaned up and eat a pasta lunch in the Officers' Mess. After a strenuous morning you are encouraged to use this meal as an opportunity to fuel and fully hydrate your body prior to the afternoon's activities.

IT IS ESSENTIAL THAT YOU EAT AND DRINK AS MUCH AS YOU CAN THROUGHOUT THE COURSE, OTHERWISE YOUR BODY WILL RUN OUT OF FUEL.

1130 – LECTURETTE

For a Royal Marines Officer, the ability to communicate with others is vital. With this in mind, you will be expected to deliver a three-minute lecturette to your fellow course members in a classroom. The subject will be the same for all candidates – Yourself – and you will not be allowed to use visual aids during the lecturette. The lecturette is designed to allow the POC staff to assess your ability to articulate and project your views confidently to a small audience. Careful planning is needed to do yourself justice in only three minutes.

1230 – ENDURANCE COURSE

Following another quick change you will be taken to the local training area on Woodbury Common, three miles from Lympstone, for the start of the Endurance Course at 1300 hrs. The course – one of the Commando Tests – consists of a run of six and a half miles over varying terrain. The first two and a half miles will be run as a group over rough ground, including water pools and 5 sets of tunnels. There will be regular pauses for an explanation of how to tackle each obstacle. This is followed by a 'Hare and Hounds' race over one mile, where you will attempt to catch up with a member of the Training Team running at the front of the group.

The final three miles are conducted as a squad run through the lanes back to CTCRM at 8 minute mile pace, don't be surprised if the pace quickens towards the end. The Endurance Course tests exactly what the title suggests.

Throughout, you will have to show not just physical fitness but the mental desire to keep going despite increasing fatigue.

1530 – DISCUSSION EXERCISE

The final assessed activity on the POC is the Discussion Exercise, which takes place back in the Officers' Mess. Controversial and topical issues are put forward for the group to debate. You are expected to participate fully and explain the reasoning behind the comments you make and expand upon other members' ideas. In this exercise we are observing your interpersonal skills, how you articulate your point of view, how you listen to others and how you react to someone who disagrees with you. Remember that if you do not become involved, it is difficult for the assessors to form a view on your qualities in this area.

By 1630 the formally assessed phase of the course is complete. The rest of the afternoon and evening is spent cleaning the equipment you were issued on Monday and relaxing and enjoying the comforts of the Mess.

1800 – DRINKS IN THE OFFICERS' MESS

Unless the Young Officer batch is training away from Lympstone, the second day ends with a chance to meet Young Officers currently under training. Over a drink or two in the Mess, they will tell you at first hand about the challenges and rewards of training.

Make the most of the opportunity to talk to them. If you do, you will get more of a flavour of what might lie ahead if you pass the POC. After dinner the rest of the evening is free. It is wise to get an early night before the third day.

DAY THREE
0800 – BATTLE SWIMMING TEST

The first event of the final day is the Battle Swimming Test. Your performance in this test is not assessed; it is included in the POC so you can gain an insight into other physical aspects of training. Although swimming can be taught at CTCRM in training, it is beneficial for you to arrive with some ability particularly at breaststroke. If not a strong swimmer, a candidate should consider swimming lessons.

0900 – PRESENTATIONS

Next follows a comprehensive presentation that concentrates on Royal Marines Young Officer training. You will also be briefed on Royal Marines careers, specialisations and methods of entry.

1030 – FINAL INTERVIEW

The POC ends with a final interview in which the Course Officer will give you your POC result. He will take you through your strengths and weaknesses as they have emerged over the past 48 hours, informing you whether:

- You have been recommended to attend AIB.
- You are advised to come back on another POC, for a further attempt, after a period of time.
- You have been assessed as unsuitable for a commission in the Royal Marines.

Whatever the outcome, you will receive a comprehensive brief from the Course Supervisor on your performance throughout the course. He will identify areas of strengths and weaknesses which will be used to formulate a future individual training programme. After the interview, by about midday, you will be free to leave. However, you are welcome to stay for lunch.

FREQUENTLY ASKED QUESTIONS ABOUT THE POC

Q. Can I bring my own boots? NB: POC ONLY NOT PRMC.

Yes, so long as they are of a military style, have a substantial heel block and adequate ankle support. All boots will be checked on day one and military boots will be issued if required.

Q. Can I use visual aids for my lecturette?

No. The use of visual aids often results in candidates failing to engage effectively with the audience. They are trying to assess candidates' ability to articulate and project their views to a small audience. Visual aids often provide a distraction to both the candidate and his audience.

Q. Will I automatically fail the course if I do not complete a test?

The POC exists to identify potential. The instructors will consider a candidate's overall performance throughout the course, however there are a number of criteria tests: Level 11 on the "bleep test", 180 (160 for scholars) on the RMFA, failure to complete one pull-up means it is unsafe to progress to Day 2, failure to conduct any of the high obstacle confidence tests, failure to complete the run back to camp after the endurance course. A candidate may fail the POC if he does not demonstrate the required levels of determination and motivation.

Q. Why do we need to carry our water bottles (issued at POC) all the time?

The physical intensity of the POC is such that it is essential to hydrate continuously. While dehydration is a concern during the warmer months, your body works best when it is fully hydrated whatever the time of year.

Q. Why has my Bleep Test result been lower than I have previously achieved at home/school?

Many Bleep Tests are run using cassette tapes that have become stretched over time. At the POC, only official Bleep Test CDs are used. Furthermore, the effect of candidates' natural apprehension, before undertaking physical tests in a strange environment, should not be underestimated.

A copy of the Bleep Test can be found here:

www.How2Become.com

HINTS AND TIPS FOR PASSING THE POC

The POC is a hard physical test. Do not underestimate the fitness required before arriving. Complete at least one run per week in boots two months prior to your course to allow your legs chance to adapt. As well as training for the RMFA it is important to increase the distance you run to prepare for the Endurance Course, as you will be working continuously for about 2 hours, after already having completed a 2 ½ hr assault course session earlier in the day.

Be aware that running in boots is harder than in trainers. To run 8 min miles in boots, you must train at a faster pace in trainers – around 7 min mile pace.

Eat well before, during and after your training sessions, and especially when you are on course, as candidates have been known to collapse due to low blood sugar levels.

If you get an injury before the POC, let it heal properly. It is better to arrive slightly less fit and not injured, than with an injury, as this may be exacerbated whilst at CTCRM.

Learn about the Royal Marines before you arrive. Consider it like any job interview – you will be expected to answer questions on the Royal Marines, Commando Units and jobs you are likely to do after joining.

THE ADMIRALTY INTERVIEW BOARD

The AIB is designed to assess whether you have the right personal qualities and attributes to become a successful Royal Marines Officer. The only way you will pass it is through hard work and determination.

There are two key elements to passing the AIB:
1. How you perform.
2. How you behave.

Whilst there are many different factors that can influence each element, they both must be taken seriously. For example, during one of the evenings at the AIB you will be allowed to visit the bar and mix with young Officer Recruits who are part way through their training. This is not a time to get drunk and let your hair down, but a time to relax and find out as much as you can about the training you will undertake if you are to be successful at the AIB. Whilst an evening in the bar is not assessable, how you behave certainly is!

The Board will naturally expect you to have found out as much as you can about the Royal Navy and the Royal Marines, and they will ask you questions about ships and equipment and your chosen specialisation so make sure you are fully prepared. It is also a good idea for you to have looked for opportunities with responsibility and personal development. Just because you are applying to become a Royal Marines Officer, it does not mean you can neglect your knowledge of the Royal Navy in general.

THE BIOGRAPHICAL QUESTIONNAIRE
Before you arrive at the AIB you will be sent a questionnaire to complete. This is used to inform the interviewers and to provide initial evidence; it is important that you complete this form as fully and accurately as possible. This is your chance to "blow your own trumpet" so to speak. Make sure you put yourself across in a positive manner and let them know about your achievements to date and anything else that you are currently involved in.

In order to assist you during your preparation, I have now provided you sample responses to a number of the biographical questionnaire questions.

SAMPLE RESPONSES (SUCCESSFUL APPLICATION)

Q. Briefly describe why you wish to become an officer in the RN, RM or RFA.

I want the challenge which comes with joining the Armed Forces would give me: to achieve what I would not otherwise expect or find myself able to achieve. I've always chosen to work in teams as I flourish as a committed team member. I've been deeply impressed by the camaraderie of service personnel.

I want to make use of my past experience as a leader – especially training and motivating people. I want to contribute to and support the work of our nation's service personnel, specifically the Royal Marines as I could commit to the RN's ethos and practice.

Q. Describe a time when you have been in charge of a project or have had to lead a team, and what you did.

When my manager left the company in 2005 I was initially given his role temporarily. It was my task to maintain all services within the company until a new manager was appointed. My priorities were: delegation, communication and motivation. I set up and led a monthly meeting of all the supervisors together from the company, as well as a weekly contact with each employee within my team. I appointed one of the supervisors to act as the point of contact for all members of staff in case they needed support during the interim period. I asked each of the other supervisors to take responsibility for organising elements of their own team and stated that I would be the point of contact for them if they needed advice, guidance or assistance.

Once this new administrative system was in place, my priority was to motivate the supervisors and staff, especially during crises and setbacks.

Q. Describe a time when you have been part of a team, including details of your own role within that team.

In 2008 I was one of four crew on a 48 foot yacht sailing from the Azores to Plymouth. None of us crew had previously sailed offshore, non-stop, that distance; nor had we previously met each other. The skipper divided us into two groups so we could 'hot bunk' the berths, and we worked watches day and night. We four crew shared on a rota basis the responsibilities of: navigation; sail trimming; keeping watch; helming (no self-steering gear on board); weather forecasting; washing up; cleaning cabins, the galley and the heads. The weather varied from no wind at all to Force 9, gusting Force 10 (during which I was the only crew who volunteered to helm). I'd recently passed the RYA Ocean Yacht master course (theory) so was able to practice some astronavigation.

Q. Describe a time when you have set yourself a challenging goal or target and endeavoured to achieve it, including information on the outcome.

In 2006 I decided that I wanted to raise money for a local charity. The aim was to raise £10,000 in total. In order to achieve this, I set myself the challenge of completing an iron-man challenge which included swimming 2 kilometres, running a marathon before finally cycling 120 miles, all in one day. I started out by planning my training routine and decided that I would need 6 months to complete the task. I gradually increased my distances over time and ensured that I ate healthily and avoided alcohol and junk food in the build-up to my challenge. I used an action plan that determined when I would train. Whilst training, I also took control of fundraising, writing to large local companies requesting sponsorship. The end result was that I completed the challenge in 9 hours and 43 minutes, raising £10,784 in the process for a local children's charity.

Let's now take a look at the AIB and what each day consists of.

DAY ONE AIB

Once the brief is completed you will then be split up into groups of 3 or 4 depending on the size of the overall group. You'll be asked to write one essay from a choice of five or six topics, usually including military, political and contemporary media issues. You will be assessed on your ability to produce logical, fluent, convincing and accurate work, not your beliefs or opinions.

After the essay, you will be taken to the gym and briefed on the Day 2 leadership tasks and the equipment used. The last part of the day, you will have the opportunity work through a sample planning exercise scenario to help prepare you for the exercise on Day 2.

The remainder of the day you will be free to take the opportunity to get to know the other members of your team whom you will be working with closely on Day 2.

DAY TWO AIB

On the morning you will get up at approx 6.15am. The first assessment you are required to sit will be the Planning Exercise in the examining room at 7.30am so it is best to get an early night the evening before. After the Planning Exercise session, you will head to the gym for the Leadership Assessment, consisting of the Team Task and Individual Leadership Task. These two assessments will commence at 09.15am until 10.30am.

After the gym activities are complete, you will be required to sit the psychometric tests, which include Verbal, Numerical and Abstract Reasoning tests. Included in this session will be your Interview with the board. The last task of the day will be the fitness test which requires you to undertake a 2,4km run on Astroturf which you will need to pass the required standard for your age/gender. Please be aware failure to reach the required standard will result in you not being forwarded for selection.

THE QUALITIES REQUIRED TO BECOME A ROYAL MARINES OFFICER

Many candidates who attend the Admiralty Interview Board will be under-prepared. In addition to this, many candidates will spend hours scouring internet chat forums in an attempt to find hints and tips on how to pass the AIB. Whilst there is nothing wrong with this, the most effectively prepared candidates are those who concentrate primarily on demonstrating the key assessable qualities in order to become a Royal Marines Officer.

The whole purpose of the AIB is to determine whether or not you have the 'potential' to become a Royal Marines Officer. If you have the potential then there is a greater chance that you will pass the Initial Training Course. The Royal Marines will be investing literally hundreds of thousands of pounds into your development and career progression. Therefore, they want to be sure that you have the potential to pass every stage of training.

In order to assess the potential, the Royal Marines will assess you against a series of qualities and competencies. Before I move on to the scoring criteria, I want to talk a little about the qualities that you need to demonstrate during the entire selection process. You will notice that after each list of qualities I have provided you with some useful tips.

Qualities that you need to demonstrate:

• Determination	• Steady
• Resolute	• Able to overcome most difficulties
• Persistent	
• Unwavering	• Strong-willed

TIPS:

You are applying to join the Royal Marines as an Officer. Therefore, it is crucial that you are able to remain calm in a crisis, be totally focused on achieving the end result and be determined to succeed at everything you do.

For example, during the planning exercise stage you will be placed under considerable pressure by the assessing Officers. If you do not know the answer to a question, then it is better to say so, rather than panic, waffle or crumble under the pressure. One of the main purposes of the Admiralty Interview Board is to determine whether or not you have the ability to stay focused under pressure.

• Imaginative • Initiative • Constructive • Perceptive • Original • Mentally agile	• Inventive • Visionary • Intelligent • Mature • Balanced

TIPS:

These qualities are predominantly focused on your state of mind. Do you have the ability to come up with solutions to problems? Can you think outside the box? Can you see the end result? Are you sensible and mature for your years? During every stage of the AIB make sure you remain level-headed. Do not act in a foolhardy way and always think before you speak. Engage your brain before you engage your mouth!

• Forceful • Compelling • Persuasive • Powerful • Vigorous • Assertive • Consistent	• Effective • Resourceful • Magnetic • Inspiring • Considerate • Considerable impact

TIPS:

Let us assume that you are participating in the Planning Exercise phase. You have worked hard during your preparation in the build up to the AIB and you are very confident that your plan of tackling the exercise is the most effective. However, two other members of your group have alternative solutions to the problem. What do you do? The options are simple – you can either go along with their desired solutions(s) or you can have the confidence in your own abilities and your plan and attempt to 'persuade' them both that your option is the most effective. If I was attending the AIB, I would have the confidence in my own abilities and persuade them that my option is the most effective.

Remember – you are applying to become a Royal Marines Officer and that means you are applying to become a leader!

• Bold	• Daring
• Courageous	• Diligent
• Entrepreneurial	• Industrious
• Enthusiastic	• Persevering
• Spirit of adventure	• Physically strong and active
• Untiring	• Organiser
• Energetic	• Sense of urgency
• Active	

TIPS:
During Practical Leadership Task (PLT), be sure to get involved. Those people, who believe that if they sit on the fence and dwon't get involved will go unnoticed, are sorely mistaken. You must get involved, come up with solutions, encourage the team, support others and try your hardest to achieve every task that you are set. When it is your turn to take command, do so.

Do not be weak; be strong, confident and in control at all times.

• Tolerant	• Tactful
• Flexible	• Resilient (never gives in)
• Co-operative	• Adaptable
• Diplomatic	• Willing to accept responsibility

TIPS:
What are you like towards other people? Do you have the ability to work with others as part of a team? Every team encounters problems along the way. How you deal with those problems is what matters. Be tolerant of other people, always be flexible in your approach to tasks, never give in and be the first to put your hand up when they ask for a volunteer.

• Sensible	• Discerning
• Respective	• Fair
• Shrewd	• Unbiased
• Well-balanced	• Loyal
• Decisive	• Steadfast

I have now provided you with plenty of qualities that all go towards making an effective Royal Marines Officer. So, when the interview panel asks you the question "What are the qualities of a Royal Marines Officer?" you will have no problem answering it!

YOU ARE A LEADER AND A MANAGER

Royal Marines Officers are both leaders and managers. Therefore, it is important that you understand the difference between each of them and how they are interlinked.

In order to become a competent RM Officer, you will need to be effective at both. Here's a brief explanation of how they differ:

LEADER – A leader is someone who effectively takes a team of people from point A to point B. These two 'points' don't have to be in terms of distance, but instead they could be a mission or a company or organisational goal. For example, it might be a football manager attempting to lead his or her team to promotion to a higher league. A leader should be a visionary. They should 'see' where they want their team to be and take steps to get them there.

MANAGER – A manager is someone who arranges and uses resources in order to achieve a companies or organisations goal. Examples of resources are:
• People;
• Utilities such as water, gas and electricity;
• Vehicles and equipment;
• Paper and pencils;
• Fuel;
• Time.

An effective manager will use his or her resources effectively. They will not waste resources and they will use them appropriately. A manager's greatest asset is his/her people whom which they command. When you join the Royal Marines as an Officer you will undoubtedly be responsible at some point in your career for a group or team of people. How you manage them is very important.

HOW DO THEY WORK TOGETHER?

During my time in the fire service, I served as an Officer for many years. Without wishing to blow my own trumpet, I was a highly effective manager and leader. Managerial and leadership skills are interlinked and you will draw on each of these assets at different times during your career as a Royal Marines Officer. For example, whilst attending severe fires and road traffic collisions in the Fire Service, I was required to use both leadership and managerial skills at the same time in order to achieve the required task. I would always have a plan that was discussed with my Junior Officers. I would assign people and equipment (resources) to carry out certain tasks at the incident. I would order equipment, fuel and refreshments (resources) well in advance of them running out. I would arrange many hours in advance for relief crews to attend the incident in order to replace my tiring firefighters. I would support my team and I would communicate effectively with them during every stage of the incident. At the end of the incident I would always hold an incident debrief. This would allow me to thank everyone for their efforts and allow us to identify any areas of improvement for future incidents.

All of these actions were using my 'managerial' skills. In terms of leadership skills, I would brief my team well in order to explain the plan and what it was that needed to be done. I would provide words of support and encouragement throughout the operation and I would listen carefully to my junior officer's advice and suggestions during every stage of the incident.

Being an Officer in the Royal Marines is about drawing on different skills and assets in order to achieve a task or goal. That goal may take many years to achieve and may not necessarily be a short term objective. Always remember that in order to become a competent Royal Marines Officer, you will need to be an effective leader and manager.

Chapter 3
The RM Officer Filter Interview

During the selection process you will be required to sit interviews at the Armed Forces Careers Office (AFCO), the Potential Officer Course (POC) and finally at the Admiralty Interview Board (AIB).

Whilst the questions and tips contained within this section of the guide concentrate primarily on the AFCO interview, they are also great preparation for the POC and AIB too. The interview, which is held at your local Armed Forces Careers Office, will be undertaken by a member of the Royal Marines recruitment team. The purpose of this interview is to 'filter' out those people who have the potential to become an RM Officer. If you have the potential, then you will get put forward to attend the POC.

The duration of the initial AFCO interview will very much depend on your responses to the questions. However, you can expect the interview to last for approximately 30 minutes. The questions that you will be assessed against during the initial interview will normally be taken from the following areas:

- The reasons why you want to join the Royal Marines and why you have chosen this service over the Army and the Royal Air Force;
- Why you want to become a Royal Marines Officer and what skills, qualities and experiences you have that would help you to become a competent Officer;
- What choice of career you are most interested in, the reason for choosing that career, and the skills you have to match the role;
- What information you already know about the Royal Navy/Royal Marines, its history, its ethos, its lifestyle and training;
- Information relating to your hobbies and interests including sporting / team activities;
- Any personal responsibilities that you currently have at home, in your education or at work;
- Information about your family and your partner and what they think about you joining;
- Information based around your initial application;
- Your experience of work and education;
- Your emotional stability and your maturity;
- Your drive and determination to succeed;
- Having a positive reaction to a disciplined environment and towards people in positions of authority.

Before I move on to a number of sample interview questions and responses I want to explain a little bit about interview technique and how you can come across in a positive manner during the interview. During my career in the Fire Service I sat on many interview panels assessing people who wanted to become firefighters. As you can imagine there were some good applicants and there were also some poor ones. Let me explain the difference between a good applicant and a poor one.

A GOOD APPLICANT
A good applicant is someone who has taken the time to prepare. They have researched both the organisation they are applying to join and also the role that they are being interviewed for. They may not know every detail about the organisation and the role but it will be clear that they have made an effort to find out important facts and information. They will be well presented at the interview and they will be confident, but not over confident. As soon as they walk into the interview room they will be polite and courteous and they will sit down in the interview chair only when invited to do so. Throughout the interview they will sit up right in the chair and communicate in a positive manner. If they do not know the answer to a question, they will say so and they won't try and waffle. At the end of the interview they will ask positive questions about the job or the organisation before shaking hands and leaving.

A POOR APPLICANT
A poor applicant could be any combination of the following. They will be late for the interview or even forget to turn up at all. They will have made little effort to dress smart and they will have carried out little or no preparation. When asked questions about the job or the organisation they will have little or no knowledge. Throughout the interview they will appear to be unenthusiastic about the whole process and will look as if they want the interview to be over as soon as possible. Whilst sat in the interview chair they will slouch and fidget. At the end of the interview they will try to ask clever questions that are intended to impress the panel.

Earlier on in this guide I made reference to a 'mock interview'. I strongly advise that you try out a mock interview before the real thing. You'll be amazed at how much your confidence will improve. All you need to do is get your parents or a friend to sit down with you and ask you the interview questions that are contained within this guide. Try to answer them as if you were at the real interview. The more mock interviews you try the more confident you'll become.

INTERVIEW TECHNIQUE

How you present yourself during the interview is important. Whilst assessing candidates for interviews I will not only assess their responses to the interview questions but I will also pay attention to the way they present themselves. A candidate could give excellent responses to the interview questions but if they present themselves in a negative manner then this can lose them marks.

Take a look at the following diagrams which indicate both poor technique and good technique.

POOR INTERVIEW TECHNIQUE

The candidate appears to be too relaxed and casual for an interview.

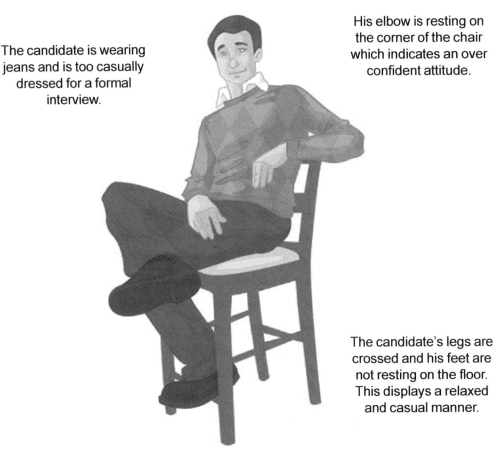

His elbow is resting on the corner of the chair which indicates an over confident attitude.

The candidate is wearing jeans and is too casually dressed for a formal interview.

The candidate's legs are crossed and his feet are not resting on the floor. This displays a relaxed and casual manner.

GOOD INTERVIEW TECHNIQUE

The candidate is smiling and he portrays a confident, but not over confident manner.

The candidate is dressed wearing a smart suit. It is clear that he has made an effort in his presentation.

His hands are in a stable position which will prevent him from fidgeting. He could also place his hands palms facing downwards and resting on his knees.

He is sitting upright in the interview chair with his feet resting on the floor. He is not slouching and he portrays himself in a positive manner.

In the build up to your initial AFCO interview practice a few 'mock' interviews. Look to improve your interview technique as well as working on your responses to the interview questions.

Now let's take a look at a number of sample interview questions. Please note that these questions are not guaranteed to be the exact ones you'll come up against at the real interview, but they are great starting point in your preparation. Use the sample responses that I have provided as a basis for your own preparation. Construct your answers on your own opinions and experiences.

SAMPLE INTERVIEW QUESTION NUMBER 1

Q. Why do you want to join the Royal Marines?

This is an almost guaranteed question during the Officer Filter interview so there should be no reason why you can't answer it in a positive manner. Only you will know the real reason why you want to join but consider the following benefits before you construct your response:

- A career in the Royal Marines is challenging. You will face challenges that are not usually available in normal jobs outside of the Armed Forces. These challenges will make you a better person and they will develop you into a professional and competent member of a proud organisation;
- A career in the Royal Marines will not only give you the chance to develop your skills and potential but it will also give you excellent qualifications and training;
- A career in the Royal Marines will give you the chance to travel and see different cultures. This alone will broaden your horizons and make you a more rounded person;
- The Royal Navy/Marines, like the other Armed Forces, is an organisation that people have a huge amount of respect for. Therefore those people who join it are very proud to be a part of such a team.

Try to display a good level of motivation when answering questions of this nature. The Royal Marines are looking for people who want to become a professional member of their team and who understand their way of life. It should be your own decision to join and you should be attracted to what this career has to offer. If you have been pushed into joining by your family then you shouldn't be there. Please see below a sample response to this question.

<u>Sample Response</u>

'I have been working towards my goal of joining the Royal Marines as an Officer for a number of years now. A couple of years ago a careers advisor visited our school to talk about the Royal Navy. After his presentation I went up to him and asked a few questions about the different career options that were available. In particular I was most interested in the Royal Marines as an Officer as I believe I have the leadership and management potential to succeed in this role. Since that day I have set my sights on joining this organisation and I have been working hard to improve myself. To be honest, I want a career that will give me direction, professional training, qualifications and the chance to work with people who set themselves very high standards. I have spoken to a friend who already works in the Royal Marines as an Officer and he fully recommends it.

I've looked at the different career options outside of the Royal Marines and nothing matches up to the challenge or the sense of pride I would feel by joining a team like this. I am the Captain of the school Rugby squad and being part of a winning team is something that I very much enjoy. Even though I am quite capable of working on my own I much prefer to work in a team where everyone is working towards the same goal. Finally, even though I have a good stable home life I can't wait to leave home and see what's out there. Even though travelling isn't the be all and end all, I am looking forward to visiting different countries and experiencing varied cultures. Many of my friends have never been out of their home town but that's not for me. I want to broaden my skills and get some decent training in the process and I believe that I would be a great asset to the Royal Marines.'

SAMPLE INTERVIEW QUESTION NUMBER 2

Q. Why have you chosen the Royal Navy/Royal Marines over the Army or the Royal Air Force?

As you know, there are three main forces that you can apply to join. The Royal Navy/Royal Marines is different to the other forces in the way that you may be required to serve on board ship for many months of your career. To some, this is not appealing. Personally I enjoyed my time on board ship. You need to be fully comfortable with this fact and be 100% certain that you can cope with the demands of living on board. Personally I believe there is nothing better than being on board a ship.

The Royal Marines will give you so much variety and it will also give you many different career options. As an Officer you will receive the highest standard of training available.

Take a look at the following sample response to this question before creating your own based on your own views and opinions.

<u>Sample Response</u>

'I did consider the other forces and even had a chat with each of the careers advisors but at the end I was still set on the Royal Marines. I even sat down with my parents and we wrote down the benefits of each of the different services and the Royal Marines came out on top in all aspects. I have always had a keen passion to work in intelligence and it is my intention to become an Officer. During my research I visited a Royal Marines base and I was fascinated at the professionalism, the history and the comradeship that I witnessed. I very much want to be part of that.

I have thought long and hard about my choice of career and I am fully aware of the training that I will undergo if I am successful. I've been working hard to pass the selection process and the Admiralty Interview Board and I am 100% certain that the Royal Marines is for me. If I am unsuccessful at this attempt, then I will look at what I need to improve on and work hard for next time.'

SAMPLE INTERVIEW QUESTION NUMBER 3

Q. What does your family think of you wanting to join the Royal Marines?

What your family think about you wanting to join is very important, simply for the reason that you will need their support both during your training and during your career. I can remember my parents being fully behind my decision to join the Royal Navy and I'm glad that they were for a very good reason. After about two weeks into my basic training I started to feel a little bit home sick; like any young man would do being away from home for a long period of time. I rang my father and discussed with him how I felt. After about five minutes talking to him I felt perfectly fine and I no longer felt home sick. During that conversation he reminded me how hard I had worked to get a place on the course and that he and my mother wanted me to succeed. For that reason alone I was glad that I had the support of my parents.

Before you apply to join the Royal Marines it is important that you discuss your choice of career with either your parents or your guardian. If you have a partner, then obviously you will need to discuss this with them too. If they have any concerns whatsoever, then I would advise you take them along with you to the Armed Forces Careers Office so they can discuss these concerns with the trained recruitment staff. Get their full support as you may need it at some point during your career, just like I did!

There now follows a sample response to help you prepare.

Sample Response

'Before I made my application I discussed my choice of career with both my parents and my girlfriend. Initially they were apprehensive but they could see how motivated and excited I was as I explained everything I had learnt so far about the service. I showed them the recruitment literature and we even planned a trip to the Royal Marines museum in Portsmouth so they could see what I would be joining. I understand that it is important they support me during my application and I now have their full backing. In fact, they are now more excited about the fact I'll be leaving home than I am! I have also told them everything I know about the training I will go through and the conditions I will serve under. They are aware that the Royal Marines has a brilliant reputation and this has helped them to further understand why I want to join.'

SAMPLE INTERVIEW QUESTION NUMBER 4

Q. What grades did you achieve at school and how do you feel about them?

Questions that relate to your education are common during the Officer selection interview. In addition to this question they may also ask you questions that relate to which schools or educational establishments you attended.

This kind of question is designed to assess your attitude to your grades and also how hard you worked whilst at school, college or university. As you can imagine, your grades will generally reflect how hard you worked and therefore you will need to be totally honest in your response. Naturally you must meet the minimum eligibility requirements for becoming an Officer in the Royal Marines before you can apply, but how well you did at school or university academically, might be a reflection as to how well you will do during initial and on-going officer training. If your results were not as good as you anticipated, then you will need to provide a good reason for this. If you achieved the grades you wanted during education, then congratulations, you'll find this question easier to answer.

Take a look at the following sample response which is tailored towards a person who did not do as well as they wished.

Sample Response

'To be totally honest I didn't do as well as I had hoped. The reason for this was that I didn't work hard enough during the build up to the exams. I did put in some preparation but I now realise I should have worked harder.

Whilst I passed the exams I know that I could have done a lot better. I fully appreciate that I will have several exams and assessments to pass during initial officer training and I have been preparing for this. I have embarked on an evening class at my local college to maintain my competence in Maths and English, and I am constantly studying Royal Navy and Royal Marines facts and history. My current affairs knowledge is excellent and I have been enjoying the study time immensely. I can assure you that, even though I should have done better at school, I have learnt from this and I am working very hard to prepare for RM Officer training in the anticipation that I am successfuil at AIB.'

SAMPLE INTERVIEW QUESTION NUMBER 5

Q. What responsibilities do you have either at work, school or at home?

When you join the Royal Marines as an Officer you will need to take full responsibility for yourself, your team, your equipment and also for the safety of your work colleagues. At the age of 18 I was responsible for servicing and maintaining Sea Harrier jets on board HMS Invincible. I was responsible for going out on deck at 4am and servicing the ejector seats that formed part of the pilot's safety equipment. That was a huge amount of responsibility to undertake.

Whatever branch you decide to join, you will need to demonstrate during selection that you can handle responsibility.

The most effective way to do this is by providing the interviewer with an example of where you have already held positions of responsibility either at home, work or during your education.

Take a look at the following sample response to this question.

Sample Response

'I currently hold a large number of responsibilities both at home and in my part-time job. I am responsible for cleaning the house top to bottom once a week and I usually do this on a Sunday before I go and play football for my local team. I'm also captain of the football team which means I have to arrange the fixtures, book the football ground and I also collect the kit at the end of the match and get it washed and dried for the following week. I also take control of the club's financial affairs as I have an interest in accountancy. I thoroughly enjoy this responsibility and would not have it any other way; I am always the first to volunteer for any task or role that involves a level of responsibility. In addition to this I have just started a new part-time job at my local supermarket as a junior supervisor. This involves managing five members of staff, managing stock levels and also managing resources. It is essential that I make sure the store has sufficient resources to operate effectively everyday that it is open.

I enjoy taking on responsibility as it gives me a sense of achievement. I understand that I will need to be responsible during my Royal Marines Officer training not only for myself, but also for ensuring that I work hard to pass every assessment in order to develop into a competent Royal Marines Officer.'

SAMPLE INTERVIEW QUESTION NUMBER 6

Q. How do you think you will cope with the discipline, regimentation and routine in the Royal Marines?

When you join the Royal Marines you will be joining a military organisation that has set procedures, standards and discipline codes. Procedures, standards and discipline codes are there for a very good reason. They ensure that the organisation operates at its best and without these, much could go wrong. As an Officer you will have the added responsibility of ensuring those underneath your command respect these important codes of conduct and policies. To some people these important aspects of service life will come as a shock when they join. The recruitment staff will want to know that you are fully prepared for this change in lifestyle. They are investing time, effort and resources into your training so they want to know that you can cope with their way of life.

When answering this type of question you need to demonstrate both your awareness of what Royal Marines life involves and also your positive attitude towards the disciplined environment. Study the recruitment literature and visit the careers website to get a feel for the type of training you will be going through.

Sample Response

'I believe I would cope with it very well. In the build up to selection I have been trying to implement routine and discipline into my daily life. I've been getting up at 6am every weekday and going on a 5 mile run.

This will hopefully prepare me for the early starts that I'll encounter during training. I've also been learning how to iron my own clothes and I've been helping around the house with the cleaning and washing. I already have to follow and manage codes of conduct in my part-time job. Being responsible for five members of staff I am required to monitor their performance, brief them on new policies and procedures, and also carry out annual appraisals.

I fully understand that the Royal Marines needs a disciplined workforce if it is to function as effectively as it does. As an Officer it is even more important that you can look after yourself as you will be a role model for the men under your command. Without discipline much could go wrong and if I did not carry out my duties professionally then I could endanger somebody's life. I am also aware that I will be required to manage discipline within my team once I am a qualified officer. I am fully prepared for this and would carry out my duties diligently, professionally and competently.'

SAMPLE INTERVIEW QUESTION NUMBER 7

Q. How do you think you will cope with being away from home and losing your personal freedom?

This type of question is one that needs to be answered positively. The most effective way to respond to it is to provide the recruitment staff with examples of where you have already lived away from home for a period of time. This could be either with your school or college, an adventure trip, camping with friends or even with a youth organisation. Try to think of occasions when you have had to fend for yourself or even 'rough it' during camps or adventure trips. If you are already an active person who spends very little time sat at home in front of the television or computer, then you will probably have no problem with losing your personal freedom. During your time in the Marines there'll be very little time to sit around doing nothing anyway. So, if you're used to being active before you join, then this is a plus.

Take a look at the sample response on the following page and try to structure your own response around this.

<u>Sample Response</u>

'I already have some experience of being away from home so I know that this would not be a problem for me. Whilst serving with the Sea Cadets I was introduced to the Navy way of life and I fully understand what it is like to be away from home. Having said that, I am not complacent and I have been working hard to improve my fitness and academic skills. To be honest with you, I'm not the kind of person who sits around at home watching television or sitting at the computer, so I'm hardly indoors anyway. In terms of losing my personal freedom I'm looking forward to the routine and regimentation that the Marines will provide as I believe this will bring some positive structure to my life. Even though I am young I want to ensure that I have a good future and I believe a career in the Royal Navy will bring me just that, providing that is, I work hard during training.

During my time in the Sea Cadets I've been away on a couple of camps and I really enjoyed this. We learnt how to fend for ourselves whilst away and I loved the fact that I was meeting new and interesting people. I understand that the training will be difficult and intense but I am fully prepared for this. I am confident that I will cope with the change in lifestyle very well.'

SAMPLE INTERVIEW QUESTION NUMBER 8

Q. Are you involved in any sporting activities and how do you keep yourself fit?

During the selection interview you will be asked questions that relate to your sporting activities and also how you keep yourself fit.

If you are the type of person who spends too much time on the computer or social networking sites, then now's the time to make a positive change. Even though you'll be on board ship there will still be time for sporting activities. Whilst on board HMS Invincible I really got into my weight training. Right at the bottom of the ship there was a small gym, and even though it was usually packed full of Royal Marines, there was still time to keep fit.

On the odd occasion when the flight deck wasn't being used for flying operations it was opened up for running and general sports such as volleyball. All of these helped to keep up the team morale on board ship.

<u>Sample Response</u>

'*I am an extremely fit and active person and I am currently involved in a couple of sports teams. To begin with, I visit the gym four times a week and carry out a light weight session before swimming half a mile in the pool.*

Sometimes I like to vary the gym session with a workout on the indoor rowing machine. In the build up to selection I have been getting up at 6am every weekday and going on a 3 mile run. This I believe will prepare me for the early starts during selection.

I am also a member of my local rugby team and I practice with them one evening a week during the season. We usually play one match a week which forms part of a Sunday league table. We are currently third in the table and are pushing hard for the top spot. Finally I am a keen hill walker and love to take off for long walks in the Lake District or Brecon Beacons with some of my friends. We usually camp out for a couple of nights over a weekend so I am used to fending for myself. I am not the type of person who just sits at home on the computer or playing video games. I love being active and always keep myself fit.'

SAMPLE INTERVIEW QUESTION NUMBER 9

Q. What do you think the qualities of a good team player are?

I have already made reference to the importance of teamwork during this guide and there is a possibility that you will be asked a question that relates to your ability to work as part of a team and also what you think the qualities of an effective team worker are. Whilst working in the Royal Marines there is a high risk that things can go wrong. You could be hundreds of miles away from base and any support from other troops could be hours away. If something serious goes wrong, then you have to work very fast and professionally as part of a team in order to resolve the issue. Before you can work effectively as a team however you need to know what the main qualities of a competent team member include. Take a look at the following:

- An ability to interact and work with others, regardless of their age, sex, religion, sexual orientation, background, disability or appearance;
- Being able to communicate with everyone in the team and provide the appropriate level of support and encouragement;
- Being capable of carrying out tasks correctly, professionally and in accordance with guidelines and regulations;
- Being focused on the team's goal(s);
- Having a flexible attitude and approach to the task;
- Putting the needs of the team first before your own;
- Putting personal differences aside for the sake of the team;
- Being able to listen to others suggestions and contributions.

When responding to this type of question it would be an advantage if you could back up your response with an example of where you have previously worked in a team. Take a look at the following sample response before creating your own based on your own experiences and ideas.

Sample Response

'A good team player must have many different qualities including an ability to listen carefully to a given brief. If you don't listen to the brief that is provided then you can't complete the task properly. In addition to listening carefully to the brief you must be able to communicate effectively with everyone in the team. As a Royal Marines Officer this will be even more important. As a team member and leader you will be responsible for supporting the other team members and listening to other people's suggestions on how a task can be achieved. You also have to be able to work with anyone in the team regardless of who they are or where they come from. You can't discriminate against anyone and if you do, then there is no place for you within that team. A good team player must also be able to carry out his or her job professionally and competently. When I say competently I mean correctly and in accordance with guidelines and training. You should also be focused on the team's goal and not be distracted by any external factors. Putting the needs of the team first is paramount. Finally a good team player must be flexible and be able to adapt to the changing requirements of the team.

I already have some experience of working in a team and I know how important it is to work hard at achieving the task. I have a job working in my local supermarket as a junior supervisor and every week we have a team briefing. During the team briefings it is my responsibility to inform the team what tasks need to be carried out as a priority. During one particular meeting I asked the team to clear a fire escape that had become blocked with cardboard boxes, debris and rubbish. In addition to this I also asked the team to come up with a plan to prevent it from happening again. Once I had briefed the team members we all set about the task carefully re-moving the rubbish. Once this was completed we then worked together in order to devise a plan to prevent it from happening again. Whilst it is important to delegate work as a leader, it is just as important to be able to work as part of that team, encourage, support and communicate as you progress through the task.'

SAMPLE INTERVIEW QUESTION NUMBER 10

Q. What do you do in your spare time?

Questions of this nature are designed to assess how effectively you use your spare time. If you are an inactive person who sits in watching television most days then you are less likely to adapt to the change in lifestyle the Marines will bring as opposed to if you are a fit, active and sporty type of person. Take a look at the following two lists which differentiate between positive ways to spend your spare time and negative ways.

POSITIVE WAYS TO SPEND YOUR SPARE TIME

- Brisk walking, running, gym work, swimming, cycling, indoor rowing;
- Studying for exams or academic qualifications;
- Preparing for a goal or aspiration such as joining the Royal Marines;
- Team activities such as football and rugby etc;
- Outdoor activities such as mountaineering, orienteering, mountain biking or climbing;
- Charity or voluntary work.

NEGATIVE WAYS TO SPEND YOUR SPARE TIME

- Sitting at home watching television or playing computer games;
- Spending hours on social networking sites;
- Sitting on park benches or being on the streets doing nothing;
- Drinking too much alcohol or smoking.

Now take a look at the following sample response to this question which will assist you in your preparation.

Sample Response

'During my spare time I like to keep active, both physically and mentally. I enjoy visiting the gym four times a week and I have a structured workout that I try and vary every few months to keep my interest up. When I attend the gym I like to work out using light weights and I also enjoy using the indoor rower. I always try and beat my best time over a 2,000 metre distance.

I'm also currently doing a weekly evening class in Judo, which is one of my hobbies. I haven't achieved any grades yet but I am taking my first one in a few weeks time. I'm also a member of the local Sea Cadets, which is an evening's commitment every week and the occasional weekend. Of course, I know when it is time to relax and usually do this by either listening to music or playing snooker with my friends but, overall, I'm quite an active person. I certainly don't like sitting around doing nothing. I understand that if I'm successful in joining the Marines, then there will be lots to keep me occupied in the evenings, especially during my basic training.'

SAMPLE INTERVIEW QUESTION NUMBER 11

Q. Can you tell me about any achievements you have experienced during your life so far?

Those people who can demonstrate a history of achievement during the Royal Marines interview are far more likely to pass the initial Officer training course. Demonstrating a history of achievement will work in your favour. Having achieved something in your life demonstrates that you have the ability to see things through to the end, something which is crucial to your career in the Marines as an Officer. It also shows that you are motivated and determined to succeed.

Try to think of examples where you have succeeded or achieved something relevant in your life. Some good examples of achievements are as follows:

- Winning a trophy with a football or hockey team;
- GCSEs, A Levels, Degrees and other educational qualifications;
- Duke of Edinburgh Award;
- Being given responsibility at work or at school;
- Raising money for charity;
- Keeping physically fit and playing team sports.

Sample Response

'Yes I can. So far in my life I have achieved quite a few things that I am proud of. To begin with I achieved good grades whilst at school in both my GCSEs and A Levels. I worked very hard to achieve my grades and I'm proud of them. At weekends I play rugby for a local team and I've achieved a number of things with them. Apart from winning the league last year we also held a charity match against the local Police rugby team. We managed to raise £500 for a local charity which was great achievement.

More recently I managed to achieve a huge increase in my fitness levels in preparation of the Bleep Fitness Test. Before I started my preparation I couldn't reach the minimum standard required but I have since worked vary hard and I can now easily pass the required target for my age group.'

SAMPLE INTERVIEW QUESTION NUMBER 12

Q. What are your strengths and what are you good at?

This is a common interview question that is relatively easy to answer. The problem with it is that many people use the same response. It is quite an easy thing to tell the interviewer that you are dedicated and the right person for the job. However, it is a different thing backing it up with evidence!

If you are asked this type of question make sure you are positive during your response and show that you actually mean what you are saying. Then, back up the strengths you have mentioned with examples of when you have been something that you say you are. For example, if you tell the panel that you are a motivated person, back it up with an example in your life where you have achieved something through sheer motivation and determination.

Sample Response

'To begin with, I'm a determined person who likes to see things through to the end. For example, I recently ran a marathon for charity. I'd never done this kind of thing before and found it very hard work, but I made sure I completed the task. Another strength of mine is that I'm always looking for ways to improve myself. As an example, I have been preparing for the Marines Officer selection process by embarking on an evening class that will see me eventually achieve a Diploma in Management Studies.

Although I have a small amount of managerial and supervisory experience, I want to make sure that I am in the best position possible for becoming a competent Royal Marines Officer. Finally, I would say that one of my biggest strengths is that I'm a great team player. I really enjoy working in a team environment and achieving things through a collaborative approach. For example, I play in a local rugby team and we recently won the league trophy for the first time since the club was established 50 years ago.'

SAMPLE INTERVIEW QUESTION NUMBER 13

Q. What are your weaknesses?

Now this is a difficult question to answer. We all have weaknesses and anyone who says they haven't is probably not telling truth. However, you must be very careful how you respond to this question. Apart from being truthful you must also provide a weakness that you are working hard on to improve. You should also remember that you are joining a disciplined service that requires hard work, determination and a will to succeed. So, if you are the type of person who cannot get up in the morning and you keep making regular mistakes at work or at school, then the Royal Marines might not be for you.

The key to responding to this type of question is to be truthful but to also back it up with examples of what you are doing to improve on your weakness.

Take a look at the following example.

Most people that know me tend to say I can sometimes overthink things.

I won't take short cuts and often find alternative ways of doing things. But this has held me back in advance, for example, I first failed the NRT, which I somewhat put down to overcomplicating the questions.

During my exams at school, I did well, but it was hard and took lots of dedication to learn question styles so that I could get the right answer in the time given, without overthinking the question.

<u>Sample Response</u>

'My biggest weakness is that sometimes I work too hard. Once I get in from my day job I am straight upstairs working on my computer, studying for the DMS course I have undertaken. Whilst being hard working is a positive aspect to my character, I do need to learn to relax and take time out. I will never be a lazy person and I really do get a lot out of working, but I must take more time to relax as this will help me to perform better when I am at work.'

SAMPLE INTERVIEW QUESTION NUMBER 14

Q. Why do you want to become an Officer? Why don't you become a Commando instead?

This type of question is designed to see if there are any genuine reasons why you have chosen to become an Officer. Some applicants get carried away with the perceived glamour and status of the role, without putting any serious thought into why they actually want to become an Officer. When preparing your response to this question you need to think about the skills and attributes that you have already gained that are relevant to the role of a Royal Marines Officer.

You may already have some genuine reasons why you want to become an Officer. Read the following sample response which will give you some good pointers when preparing for this question.

In short, yes I want to become an officer because of the added responsibility and decision making involved. But I have always, since around the age of 11, wanted to be a Royal Marine. So if unsuccessful here, I would retry as a commando but would work hard to hopefully become an officer via other avenues after progressing through the ranks. However, I am laser focused with this application and I feel I am more likely to succeed in anything I do if I don't give myself room for failure, and so wouldn't consider it unless absolutely necessary.

Sample Response

"I have thought long and hard about applying to become an Officer and I am certain that this is what I want to do. To begin with, I spent considerable time assessing my own qualities and attributes and I believe they would be most suited to that of an Officer. I am hard working, tenacious, resolute, professional, driven and ambitious and feel that these qualities will allow me to eventually become a competent Officer in the Royal Marines. In addition to my qualities I have already gained some experience in a supervisory role within my current job. I really enjoy the additional responsibility that this brings and would not thrive in a role that holds little or no responsibility.

It is my ultimate goal to join the Royal Marines and serve as an Officer. I am determined and resolute and believe that I would make an invaluable contribution to this elite service.'

SAMPLE INTERVIEW QUESTION NUMBER 15

Q. What are the different ranks for both Royal Marines Officers and Commandos?

This question assesses your knowledge of the ranks within the Royal Marines. It is a simple question and one that should be relatively easy to respond to. Having an understanding of the different ranks for both commissioned and non-commissioned staff will be an obvious advantage for when you start your initial training. You should also make yourself aware of the different rank structures for the Royal Navy. Here are the ranks within the Royal Marines for you to study:

COMMANDO TYPES

Lance Corporal

⬇

Corporal

⬇

Sergeant

⬇

Staff Sergeant

⬇

Colour Sergeant

⬇

Warrant Officer 2

⬇

Warrant Officer 1

COMMANDO OFFICER TYPES

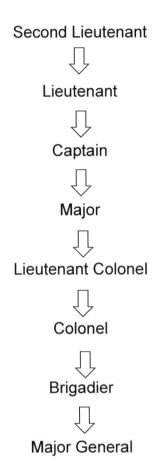

Second Lieutenant

⇩

Lieutenant

⇩

Captain

⇩

Major

⇩

Lieutenant Colonel

⇩

Colonel

⇩

Brigadier

⇩

Major General

You may also decide to study the different markings for each rank prior to your interview. These can be viewed at the official website:

www. royalnavy.mod.uk.

FURTHER SAMPLE INTERVIEW QUESTIONS

Q16. Tell me about the basic training you will undergo as an Officer.
Q17. What is the minimum service contract you will be required to sign as an Officer?
Q18. What part of RM Officer training would you find the hardest?
Q19. What have you been doing so far to prepare for the Admiralty

Interview Board?

Q20. If you fail Officer selection, would you consider joining as a Commando?   *Page 80.*

FINAL INTERVIEW TIPS

Within this section of the guide I will provide you with some final tips that will help you prepare for the Royal Marines Officer filter interview.

Remember that your success will very much depend on how prepared you are. Don't forget to work on your interview technique, carry out plenty of research and work on your responses to the interview questions.

- In the build up to the interview carry out plenty of targeted preparation work. Read your recruitment literature and spend time studying the Royal Navy/Royal Marines website. Ask the AFCO recruitment advisor to provide you with further information about the Officer training you'll undergo;
- Work on your interview technique and make sure you try out at least one mock interview. This involves getting your family or friends to sit you down and ask you the interview questions that are contained within this guide;
- When you receive your date for the interview make sure you turn up on time. Check your travel and parking arrangements the day before your interview. The last thing you need is to be late for your interview!
- Think carefully about what you are going to wear during the interview. I am not saying that you should go out and buy an expensive suit but I do recommend you make an effort to dress smartly. Having said that, if you do decide to wear a smart suit or formal outfit make sure it is clean and pressed. You can still look scruffy in a suit!
- Personal hygiene is all part and parcel of Royal Marines life. Don't attend the interview unwashed, dirty or fresh from the building site!
- When you walk into the interview room, stand up straight with your shoulders back. Project an image of confidence and be polite, courteous and respectful to the interviewer at all times;
- Don't sit down in the interview chair until invited to do so. This will display good manners;
- Whilst you are in the interview chair sit upright with your hands resting on your knees, palms facing downwards. It is OK to use your hands expressively, but don't overdo it;
- Don't slouch in the chair. At the end of each question re-adjust your

position;

- Whilst responding to the interview questions make sure you speak up and be positive. You will need to demonstrate a level of motivation and enthusiasm during the interview;
- Go the extra mile and learn a little bit about the Royal Marines history. When the panel ask you "What can you tell us about the Royal Marines?" you will be able to demonstrate that you have made an effort.

Chapter 4
The AIB Scoring Criteria

Before I go onto explain the scoring criteria, let us first of all take a look at some of the competencies required to successfully pass the Royal Marines Officer initial training course at Britannia Royal Naval College (BRNC).

COMPETENCIES REQUIRED FOR SUCCESS DURING INITIAL OFFICER TRAINING

Interpersonal Competencies

Communicating effectively	Able to communicate accurately and effectively both orally and in writing.
Teamwork	Able to work with others to achieve common goals.
Influencing	Can influence others to follow a certain course of action.

Problem Solving Competencies

Appreciation	Comprehends, identifies, extracts and assimilates information from a range of sources, quickly and accurately.
Reasoning	Thinks logically, practically and coherently to produce a successful or reasonable solution, quickly and accurately.
Organisation	Determines priorities and allocates resources effectively and efficiently to a task(s).
Capacity	Holds and processes multiple inputs whilst maintaining task performance.

Character Competencies

Decisiveness	Makes sound appropriate decisions within time-scale demanded by the situation.
Self-motivation	Demonstrates a high level of commitment and interest to tasks.
Self-analysis	Monitors and objectively analyses own performance.
Integrity	Behaviour is guided by principles, morals and ethics appropriate to service life. Adheres to rules and regulations specific to the Royal Marines.

Now that we understand some of the competencies that are required to pass Royal Marines Initial Officer Training, we can explore the type of qualities the assessors will be looking for during the Admiralty Interview Board.

EXAMPLES OF COMPETENCIES ASSESSED DURING THE ADMIRALTY INTERVIEW BOARD

Example competency	Description
Communication	• Delivers communication in a concise and effective manner, both written and orally. • Listens to others suggestions • Contributes when appropriate. • Understands the situation/ discussion.
Teamwork	• Is able to work with others in order to achieve a task or goal. • Puts in plenty of effort. • Treats others appropriately. • Supports other team members. • Communicates with the team. • Encourages the team.
Influencing	• Has considerable impact on others. • Can persuade and direct others.
Problem Solving	• Can judge certain situations. • Is flexible. • Is decisive. • Can come up with solutions to most problems.
Confidence and Resilience	• Self assured. • Is composed and calm. • Acts with a sense of urgency when required. • Can be assertive when required. • Perseveres. • Determined. • Resolute.

WHEN ARE THE COMPETENCIES ASSESSED?

Each of the qualities will be assessed during every stage of the AIB, although some more than others. For example, you will be assessed on your influencing capabilities considerably during the planning exercise and your teamwork skills during the Leadership Assessment when you are not in command.

You can begin to understand now why it is important to find out what tasks you are going to undertake during the AIB. It is important that you show and behave in accordance with the personal qualities and the core competencies being assessed.

Chapter 5
AIB Running Order and Tips

During this brief chapter I will provide you with a sample running order for the Admiralty Interview Board. It will give you a basic idea of what you will go through during your stay at the BRNC.

I have also provided you with a number of useful tips to help you prepare for each element.

THE BIOGRAPHICAL QUESTIONNAIRE

Before you arrive at the AIB you will be sent a questionnaire to complete. This helps the Royal Navy/Royal Marines make an initial assessment about you. Therefore, it is important that you complete the form as fully and accurately as possible. It is your chance to blow your own trumpet.

THE FIRST AFTERNOON (DAY ONE)

You should arrive at HMS Sultan before lunch and although day one is not a full day it is very much part of the AIB. It's your opportunity to get to know the people you'll be working with over the two days and to prepare for the tests ahead.

Upon arrival you will report to the candidates' reception and find out about where you will be living over the two days. Remember to hand in your completed biographical questionnaire. My advice is to dress smart for the AIB. You do not have to invest in an expensive designer suit, but do make the effort to look smart and informal. Personal hygiene is also very important.

After lunch you will be welcomed to the AIB by the Board president. You will be then briefed on the tasks to be undertaken in the next day and a half.

ESSAY

Following lunch at 1300 hrs you will be given 60 minutes to write about a subject chosen from a list of four topics. This assessment will assess your written communication skills. During the essay you are assessed against:

- Overall construction (e.g. paragraphing);
- Sentence construction;
- Style;
- Relevance of points and arguments;

- Vocabulary;
- Impact;
- Legibility and spelling.

TIPS FOR CREATING AN EFFECTIVE ESSAY

TIP 1
For the introduction, write the thesis statement and give some background information. The thesis statement is put into the essay introduction and it should reveal your point of view on the matter, or position you intend to support in your paper.

TIP 2
Develop each supporting paragraph and make sure to follow the correct format.

TIP 3
Write clear and simple sentences to express your meaning. Concentrate on correct grammar, punctuation and spelling. If you are unsure how to spell a specific word, avoid using it!

TIP 4
Focus on the main idea of your essay.

TIP 5
Consider using a well structured format for your essay such as:
- Beginning – Include the thesis statement and background information.
- Middle – This will be the main part of the essay and will include your argument, the reasons for it and any supporting evidence or information.
- End – Conclude and summarise. Make sure your conclusion actually concludes something and doesn't just leave you sitting on the fence, or the assessor unsure of what your actual point was.

In order to prepare for the essay, try writing one on any of the following topics:

SAMPLE ESSAY TOPIC 1
Politicians too often base their decisions on what will please the voters, not on what is best for the country.

SAMPLE ESSAY TOPIC 2
Wealthy politicians cannot offer fair representation to all the people.

SAMPLE ESSAY TOPIC 3
In a free society, laws must be subject to change.

SAMPLE ESSAY TOPIC 4
An understanding of the past is necessary for solving the problems of the present.

SAMPLE ESSAY TOPIC 5
Education comes not from books but from practical experience.

SAMPLE ESSAY TOPIC 6
Would National ID cards help prevent terrorism?

SAMPLE ESSAY TOPIC 7
Does immigration benefit the country?

SAMPLE ESSAY TOPIC 8
What will help curb gun and knife crime in the UK?

SAMPLE ESSAY TOPIC 9
Would National Service rehabilitate criminals?

PREPARATION FOR DAY 2 PRACTICAL LEADERSHIP EXERCISES (1400 – 1600)

After completion of the essay, you will change into your physical training clothes and head to the gym for a briefing and practice of the gym exercises you will undertake during Day 2. Not only will you be briefed about the Leadership tasks, you will also have the opportunity to get to grips with the equipment you will be using. Make sure you take full advantage of this session as this will be your opportunity to practice the methods used in these tasks.

PRACTICE THE PLANNING EXERCISES (1730 – 1830)

The final task of Day 1 gives you the opportunity to work through a Practice Planning Exercise. Again make the most of this opportunity. The more practice you can get the better you will perform when you are required to undertake the actual task on Day 2. After this you will have free time to get to know the other members of your group. Try to get an early night in preparation for the challenging day ahead.

THE FIRST FULL DAY (DAY TWO)

PLANNING EXERCISE

You will be provided with a written brief, containing details of a fictitious scenario. You will then have just 15 minutes to study the brief. Once the 15 minutes is up, the assessors will then introduce a problem into the scenario setting. You will then have 15 minutes to discuss possible solutions with your group and reach an agreed plan. You will then be required to present your agreed plan to the Board. Each person in the group will then be questioned in turn to examine their grasp of the situation.

TIPS

- This is probably one of the hardest elements of AIB. It is crucial that you are competent in the use of Speed, Distance and Time. Please visit the Planning Exercise section of this guide which will assist you during your preparation.
- Read the scenario thoroughly! Do not skim through it as you will miss important elements.
- Be vocal and active during the group discussion stage of the exercise. Remember the important competency of 'influencing'.
- Explain your point of view and why your plan works.
- Don't dismiss others comments directly out of hand.
- Practice by carrying out plenty of Speed, Distance and Time questions (SDT). In addition to writing down SDT calculations, you should also get someone to fire questions at you. This is far harder than sitting down and working out the answers but it will be more beneficial to you during the AIB.

- Practice SDT questions at the following website:

SpeedDistanceTime.info

LEADERSHIP ASSESSMENT (0915 – 1030)

Working in teams in the gym you are required to solve a practical problem, put a plan into action and respond to emerging difficulties. The task is designed to test your teamwork and leadership ability, your verbal powers of communication, and your resilience and strength of character.

- Be very supportive of your team.
- Be in control when you are the person in command.
- Acknowledge other's suggestions, but always be in control.
- Don't panic. It is OK to ask for suggestions.
- Think outside of the box. If an object provided is of no use to you, don't use it!

THE AIB INTERVIEW AND PSYCHOMETRIC TESTS (1100 – 1500)

During the next four hours you will sit a number of psychometric tests and be interviewed by members of the board.

The three psychometric tests will be assessing your:
- Verbal Reasoning;
- Numerical Reasoning;
- Abstract Reasoning.

AIB INTERVIEW

The competency based interview lasts for approximately 30 minutes. Whilst I have provided you with an entire section dedicated to the interview, here's a few important tips to help you prepare:

1. During your preparation, think about times when you have already been a leader or supervisor. If you have no experience in this area then it would be a good idea to go and get some.
2. Think of times when you have organised something in your life.

Write down the process that you followed from beginning to end.

3. Be able to provide examples of where you have been in a team and shown courage.
4. The assessors will ask you why you want to join the Royal Marines, your understanding of your chosen specialisation and your hopes and aspirations. They will also expect you to demonstrate your wider knowledge about the Royal Marines, and in particular to find out if it extends beyond a simple reading of the leaflets that they provide.
5. In the build up to the AIB, live and breathe the Royal Marines.
6. Be competent in current affairs before you attend the AIB. See the later chapter that relates to the AIB interview for more tips, advice and a host of sample questions.

FITNESS ASSESSMENT

After the interview and psychometric tests you will conduct a 2.4km run on Astroturf. This is a pass or fail test. If you do not reach the standard required for your age/gender you will not be forwarded for selection, irrespective of your final score.

THE RESULT

The Royal Marines will normally tell you your results individually in the afternoon of the last day. If unsuccessful, you will be free to leave. However, if you have passed, you will need to complete a medical examination. Success at the AIB does not guarantee entry into training. All successful candidates are placed in order of merit and the final selection will depend on the number of vacancies available and the number of successful candidates who reach the required medical and educational standards.

Chapter 6
The Leadership Assessment

During the Admiralty Interview Board you will be required to undertake the Leadership Assessment. The assessment is usually carried out in a gym/hangar type setting and will incorporate come kind of obstacle course. During the tasks you will be required to:

1. Be part of the team when it is not your turn to lead.
2. Act as the leader of a task during a specific task that you must resolve.

When acting as the leader it will be your responsibility to brief the team, lead them and solve a specific problem. When you are not the person leading you will need to act as a competent team player and assist the team in achieving its goal(s). Let's now take a look at how you can achieve high marks during the tasks. I will break the information down into two sections, one section for when you are acting as part of the team and one section when you are the designated leader.

WHEN ACTING AS A TEAM MEMBER

When acting as a team member you will still be assessed. Team work is an essential part of Royal Marine life, so make sure you work hard to complete the task and assist the designated leader. You should get stuck in, come up with suggestions, listen to the leader, support other team members and shout words of encouragement.

WHEN ACTING AS THE DESIGNATED LEADER

This is obviously the most important part of the assessment. It is your chance to shine as the leader so take stock of the following components and try to implement them into your turn as the leader.

Component 1 – Brief

You will be provided with a brief at the beginning of the task. It will be your responsibility to read the brief carefully, brief the members of your team and come up with a solution to the problem. Listen to the brief very carefully and communicate every element of it to the rest of your team.

Component 2 – Plan

Every team that is working towards a common goal should have a plan in place. If you don't have a plan, how are you going to achieve the task in hand? The way to compile a successful plan is to ask the team if they have any ideas on how the task could be achieved. You may however already have ideas of your own for how the problem could be solved. If so, brief your team and then go all out to achieve the task.

Component 3 – Time
It is important that any team working towards a common goal is aware of the time constraints. Make sure everyone is aware of the time and keep checking it regularly, if the facility exists. As the designated leader you may decide to appoint a dedicated timekeeper. It is crucial that you and your team act with a sense of urgency at all times.

Component 4 – Communication
This is probably the most important component of any team task. Communication means talking to, and listening to, the other members of the team. Get this part wrong and the task is guaranteed to fail. You should communicate with your team constantly.

Component 5 – Allocation of tasks
Everybody in the team will have different 'strengths'. You should try to find out who is good at what, and then allocate tasks accordingly. For example, if the task requires heavy lifting, find out who has the most strength in your team. If there are knots to be tied, is there anyone in your team capable of doing this? The phrase 'round pegs in round holes' springs to mind!

Component 6 – Support
It is the duty of every team member to support the other members of the team. You should shout words of encouragement to your team members. Whilst this may feel uncomfortable to some, if you fail to do it, you will score lower than you would otherwise. Here are a few suggestions:

- "This is great work team, keep going!"
- "Is everyone in the team OK? Let me know if there are any problems"
- "Fantastic effort team, there's not too far to go now!"

At the end of the task, make sure you congratulate your team on their efforts – this is important. Go round and speak to everyone, pat them on the back and be vocally supportive of your team.

Component 7 – URGENCY!

Regardless of how long you have to complete the task, urgency is a must. Now let's take a look at a number of tips that will help you to brief your team when you are the designated leader.

BRIEFING THE TEAM

Once you have received the brief from the assessing Officer you will have a short period of time to come up with a plan in order to achieve the task.

Here is an excellent format to follow when briefing any team in a command situation:

SMEAC

SITUATION – EXPLAIN WHAT THE SITUATION IS.
"OK, gather around team and pay attention whilst I explain the situation. Our task today is to…"

MISSION – ONCE YOU HAVE EXPLAINED THE SITUATION, TELL THE TEAM WHAT THE MISSION IS.
"Our mission is to…"

EXECUTION – TELL YOUR TEAM HOW YOU ARE GOING TO ACHIEVE THE TASK INCLUDING THE ALLOCATION OF TASKS (PLAN).
"We will achieve the task by carrying out XYZ."

ASKING QUESTIONS – ASK YOUR TEAM IF ANYONE HAS ANY QUESTIONS.
"Is the brief clear team? Does anyone have any questions?"
CHECK FOR UNDERSTANDING – CHECK TO SEE THAT YOUR TEAM FULLY UNDERSTANDS WHAT IS EXPECTED FROM THEM.
"Is everyone clear of the team task and their role within the team?"

I have used SMEAC many times in the past during training exercises and also during firefighting operations. It provides a degree of organisation to any team and I would recommend that you learn it and use it during the command task when you are the person in charge.

OK, here's a few final tips to assist you during the Leadership Assessment, both when you are a designated leader and team member.

TIP 1
When you are not the person in charge, be an effective team leader. Help out as much as possible and get stuck in! You may also wish to shout words of encouragement, to the other members of the team. "Let's keep going everyone, were doing a great job here."

TIP 2
When you are the allocated person in charge, take control of your team.
"OK everyone, gather around and pay attention to the following brief..."

TIP 3
Be supportive of your team members and get involved when necessary.

TIP 4
When briefing the team, consider using SMEAC.

TIP 5
If things start to go wrong, do not panic. Remain calm and in control. Keep going until the end and try your absolute hardest to complete the task. At the end of the task, whether it has been successful or not, thank your team for their efforts.

TIP 6
Keep an eye on safety. You are the person in charge and therefore responsible for safety.

Chapter 7
Preparing for the Planning Exercises

You will most probably find this element of the AIB the toughest. Before we look at how you can prepare effectively, here's an explanation as to what is involved.

INDIVIDUAL STUDY TIME

Each person will be provided with a copy of the brief/setting. You will then have just 15 minutes to sit in silence and read the scenario. It is important that you read everything carefully. Do not miss out any of the scenario as this could hinder you during the group discussion phase and questioning by the assessors. If you miss out anything, the assessors will pick up on it.

GROUP DISCUSSION

Once the 15 minute period is complete you will then have a period of time to discuss the scenario, and how you intend to approach it, with the other candidates in your group. During this stage make sure you are vocal and active in the construction of the plan – this is VERY important. Do not be afraid to make suggestions and if you have the confidence in your own plan, try and influence the other members of the group. Pay attention at all times, be involved and never dismiss someone's suggestions directly out of hand.

It is crucial that you are competent in the use of Speed, Distance and Time before you attend the AIB. My advice is simple:
- Practice SDT questions everyday in the build up to the AIB. You can obtain free SDT questions at the website **www.SpeedDistanceTime. info**. Although this website is primarily for RAF Officer candidates, it is perfect for those people who are attending the AIB.
- You should also practice SDT questions by having someone fire questions at you. This is a lot harder than working them out with a pen and paper!

Finally, be competent in the use of the 24-hour clock. The assessing officers will expect you to use it when answering their questions.

TOP TIPS FOR SCORING HIGH DURING THE PLANNING EXERCISE

- Demonstrate strength of character;
- Don't give in, even if things are going wrong;
- Support your decision and consider all eventualities;
- Improve general arithmetic and be competent in the use of speed, distance and time (SDT);
- Be able to calculate SDT questions in your head, as well as being able to write them down. You can practice by getting a member of your family to ask you a series of SDT questions. This is great practice as you will be under pressure to answer the questions without the use of a calculator, pen and paper;
- Keep an eye on the time. You need to come up with a solution to the problem;
- Be alert and quick to respond to questions;
- Never lie when answering questions from the assessors, they will see straight through it. If you do not know the answer to a question, then just say so;
- Always remain calm. The questioning at the end of the exercise is designed to be tough and assess how well you cope under pressure.

SPEED, DISTANCE AND TIME

Accuracy and agility in speed, distance, and time calculations will help you perform well during the Royal Marines Officer selection process. The following information will assist you in understanding how to tackle these types of question.

When trying to solve these problems it is important to consider three variables: speed, distance and time. Try not to get too worried as two of these variables will always be known. The easiest way to solve these equations is to use the following formulas:

- Speed = Distance ÷ Time

- Distance = Speed x Time

- Time = Distance ÷ Speed

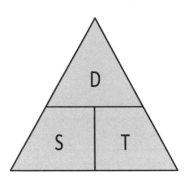

The triangular diagram above is ideal for helping you to remember the formula. Simply place your finger over the variable you are trying to discover, you will then see the equation required.

For example if you wanted to obtain the time, placing your finger on 'T' would show that you would need to divide distance (D) by speed (S).

Let's now work through some examples:

1. A train travels 60 miles in 3 hours. What is the train's speed?
Formula: Speed = distance ÷ time

Speed = 60 ÷ 3 = 20 mph

2. A car is travelling at 30 mph for 70 minutes. What is the distance travelled?

With this problem it is important to remember to work in minutes!
- So, 30 mph = 0.5 miles per minute (30 ÷ 60)
- 70 (minutes) × 0.5 = 35 miles

You can use the formula but you need to convert the minutes into hours and remember that $0.1 = \frac{1}{10}$ of 60 minutes:
FORMULA: DISTANCE = SPEED × TIME
Distance = 30 × 1.1666r (1 hour 10 mins) = 35

3. A tank is driving at 48 mph over 60 miles. How long was it driving

for?

FORMULA: TIME =DISTANCE ÷ SPEED

Time = 60 ÷ 48 = 1 hour 15 minutes Take these steps

I.   You know that 48 mph = 48 miles in 60 minutes.
II.   The difference between 60 and 48 is 12, which is ¼ of 48.
III.   You can then take ¼ of 60, which gives 15 minutes, and add that to 60 minutes = 75 minutes.
IV.   Then convert to hours = 1 hour 15 minutes for the answer!

OR

Take these steps
I.   You know that 48 mph = 0.8 miles per minute.
II.   60 ÷ 0.8 = 75 minutes.
III.   Convert into hours = 1 hour 15 minutes.

Once you understand how to calculate speed, distance and time, take your time to work through the 30 sample test questions that follow.

In order to obtain further Speed, Distance and Time questions, and also try 8 planning exercises, please go to:

www.rNOfficeraib.co.uk

For the below practice Speed, Distance and Time questions, you should write your answers using only the whole numbers! Some of these questions, will have remainders, and therefore you should only write the whole number, not the decimal!

SAMPLE SPEED, DISTANCE AND TIME QUESTIONS

Question 1
You are travelling at 28 mph for 75 minutes. How far do you travel?

1 hr   15

$$28 + \frac{28}{4} = 35 \text{ miles}$$

Question 2
You travel 15 miles in half an hour. What speed are you travelling at?

30mph

Question 3
You travel 33 miles at a constant speed of 55 mph. How long are you travelling for?

$$\frac{3}{5} = 0.6 \text{ hours} = 36 \text{ minutes}$$

Question 4
You are travelling at 75 mph for 1 and half hours. How far do you travel?

1.5

$$75 + 37.5 = 112.5 \text{ miles}$$

Question 5
You travel 61 miles in 1 hour and 5 minutes. What speed are you travelling at?

61 +

56.

$$\frac{61}{65} = \frac{61}{\times 60} \qquad 65 \overline{)3660}$$

56.30
65 ⟌3660 · 0

```
    61
  x 60
  0 0
  3660
```

```
  65
  130
  195
  260
  325
```

```
  366   390
 -325
    4·0
```

Question 6
You travel 90 miles at a constant speed of 30 mph. How long are you travelling for?

> 3 hours

Question 7
You are travelling at 70mph for 125 minutes. How far do you travel?

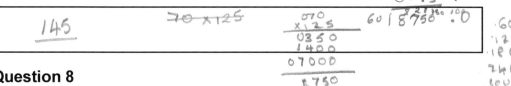

> 145

Question 8
You travel 2.5 miles in 5 minutes. What speed are you travelling at?

> $\frac{2.5}{\frac{1}{12}} = \frac{5}{2} \times 12 = \frac{60}{2} = 30 \text{ Mph}$

Question 9
You travel 75 miles at a constant speed of 45mph. How long are you travelling for?

$T = \frac{d}{s}$

$\frac{2}{3} \times 60 \quad 20$

> $\frac{75}{45} = \frac{15}{9} = \frac{5}{3} = 1.67 \text{ hours.}$
> $= 1 \text{ hour } 40 \text{ minutes.}$

Question 10
You are travelling at 59 mph for quarter of an hour. How far do you travel?

$59 \times \frac{1}{4} = 4 \overline{\smash)59 \cdot {}^30 {}^20}$

> 14.75 ~ 15   14 (Truncate).

79
158
237

Question 11
You travel 325 miles in 4 hours and 6 minutes. What speed are you travelling at?

$\frac{325}{4} + \frac{325}{\frac{1}{10}} \qquad \frac{325}{246} \times 60$

$\frac{81 \cdot 2}{4 \overline{\smash)325 \cdot 0}} \qquad \underline{325} \qquad \begin{array}{r}325 \\ -246 \\ \hline 079\end{array} \quad 1 \text{ and } \frac{79}{246} \qquad \frac{1}{3}$

> 79

60   80mph.

Question 12
You travel 38 miles at 45 mph. How long are you travelling for?

Question 13
You are travelling at 80 mph for 15 minutes. How far do you travel?

Question 14
You travel 63 miles in 56 minutes. What speed are you travelling at?

Question 15
You travel 18 miles at 50 mph. How long are you travelling for?

Question 16
You are travelling at 65 mph for one hour and 10 minutes. How far do you travel?

Question 17
You travel 120 miles in two hours. What speed are you travelling at?

Question 18
You travel 80 miles at 50 mph. How long are you travelling for?

Question 19
You are travelling at 40 mph for half an hour. How far do you travel?

Question 20
You travel 80 miles in 1 ¾ of an hour. What speed are you travelling at?

Question 21
You travel 35 miles at 70 mph. How long are you travelling for?

Question 22
You are travelling at 15 mph for 8 minutes. How far do you travel?

Question 23
You travel 16 miles in quarter of an hour. What speed are you travelling at?

Question 24
You travel 60 miles at 55 mph. How long are you travelling for?

Question 25
You are travelling at 30 mph for 10 minutes. How far do you travel?

Question 26
You travel 75 miles in one and half hours. What speed are you travelling at?

Question 27
You travel 1 mile at 60 mph. How long are you travelling for?

Question 28
You are travelling at 50 mph for 2 and half hours. How far do you travel?

Question 29
You travel 100 miles in 1 hour and 55 minutes. What speed are you travelling at?

Question 30

You travel 600 miles at 80 mph. How long are you travelling for?

answer

ANSWERS TO SAMPLE SPEED, DISTANCE AND TIME QUESTIONS

1. 35 miles	16. 75 miles
2. 30 mph	17. 60 mph
3. 36 mins	18. 1 hour 36 mins
4. 112.5 miles	19. 20 miles
5. 56 mph	20. 45 mph
6. 3 hours	21. 30 mins
7. 145 miles	22. 2 miles
8. 30 mph	23. 64 mph
9. 1 hour 40 minutes	24. 1 hour 5 mins
10. 14 miles	25. 5 miles
11. 79 mph	26. 50 mph
12. 50 mins	27. 1 minute
13. 20 miles	28. 125 miles
14. 67.5 mph	29. 52 mph
15. 21 minutes	30. 7 hours 30 minutes

On the following pages I have provided you with a sample planning exercise for you to try. Give it a go and see how you get on. There is no time limit for this sample exercise.

PLANNING EXERCISE - SEASIDE MISSION

You are the duty officer in charge at the Royal National Lifeboat Institution's (RNLI) rescue centre at FLITTERBY. The FLITTERBY lifeboat is currently involved in rescuing some sailors from a drifting yacht in the Irish Sea.

It is exactly 10:00 am and the coxswain of the lifeboat has just radioed the following message to you:

"One of the sailors we have taken off from the sinking yacht is desperately ill and must have a blood transfusion as soon as possible. I have just been talking, by radio, to the Accident & Emergency (A&E) staff at ASHBY hospital and they will be standing-by to receive him but have pointed out that every minute counts. Make sure the RNLI's ambulance (a specially adapted estate car) is ready to take him to the hospital as soon as we arrive at the jetty. I cannot give you an exact time of arrival, but it will not be before 10:20 hours, or later than 10:45 hours. Once we are tied up, it will take us 5 minutes to get him from the boat into the ambulance. It will be up to you to get him from the jetty to the A&E dept with the utmost urgency."

You study the map and recollect that there are 3 ways to get to hospital, each with advantages and disadvantages:

1. The route via the gate bridge is subject to delays as the crossings are controlled and the bridge is only open 3 times per hour for 12 minutes. The bridge is open at 10 minutes past, on the half hour and 10 minutes to the hour. The journey across the gate bridge will take you 10 minutes. The B120 is twisty and a maximum average speed could be no greater than 40 mph.
2. The route through the centre of ASHBY on the A424 is further but although it should be possible to average 40 mph out of town, once inside the central congestion zone, heavy traffic and narrow streets means no more than 5 mph can be averaged for the 10 miles through the walled part of the town. The one limitation from using the A424 is that from 11:00 hrs onwards the central congestion zone is very dense and traffic is at a standstill.
3. The new A11 by-pass is dual carriage and passes the hospital but,

although the longest route, will allow averages of 70 mph to be achieved. It is possible to reach the A11 from FLITTERBY in 10 mins.

You warn the duty driver to stand-by. Unfortunately, you cannot alert the local police on the telephone to make any special arrangements, so there is no way of interrupting the steady but reliable timetable of the gate bridge. The duty officer at nearby RAF Valley tells you the Search and Rescue helicopter is unavailable as it is on a mission rescuing someone from an oil rig miles out to sea.

Your aim is to transport the sailor to the hospital in the quickest time possible.

Question 1

How long in minutes will it take you to get from RNLI Flitterby to the A11 junction?

10 mins.

Question 2

Based on the sailor arriving at Flitterby at the earliest time possible, what time will you reach the Hospital if you choose route 1?

Question 3

Based on the sailor arriving at Flitterby at the latest time possible, what time will you reach the Hospital if you choose route 3?

Question 4

Based on the sailor arriving at Flitterby at the latest time possible, what time will you reach the Hospital if you choose route 1?

Question 5

Based on the sailor arriving at Flitterby at the earliest time possible, what time will you reach the Hospital if you choose route 2?

NOTE - You are to calculate the total journey times for each of the 3 different routes using Speed, Distance and Time calculations.   10 20

YOUR CALCULATIONS

- Speed = Distance ÷ Time

- Distance = Speed x Time

- Time = Distance ÷ Speed

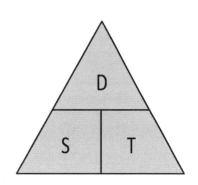

SEASIDE MISSION SKETCH

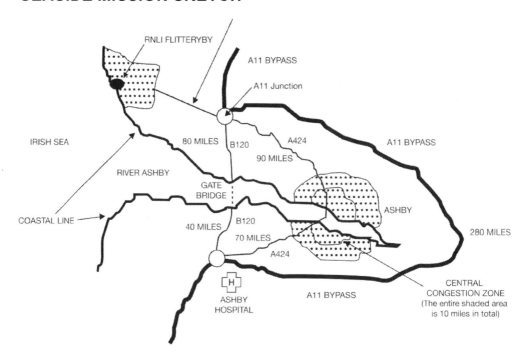

ANSWERS TO QUESTIONS

Question 1
How long in minutes will it take you to get from RNLI Flitterby to the A11 junction?

ANSWER: 10 minutes

Question 2
Based on the sailor arriving at Flitterby at the earliest time possible, what time will you reach the Hospital if you choose route 1?
The sailor arrives at Flitterby at 10:20hrs. It takes 5 minutes to load him into the ambulance which brings the time to 10:25hrs. It takes 10 minutes to get to the A11 junction which brings the time to 10:35hrs.

Travelling route 1, it is a total of 80 miles to the Gate Bridge. We are able to travel at a maximum speed of 40mph. To find out the time it takes to travel this distance we need to use the following calculation:

Time = Distance / Speed Time = 80 / 40
Answer: 2 hours

We now know that we will arrive at the Gate Bridge at 12:35hrs. From the information provided we know that the Gate Bridge is open 3 times per hour for 12 minutes. The bridge is open at 10 minutes past, 30 minutes past and 10 minutes to the hour.

The bridge is already open when we arrive at 12:35 hours; therefore we are able to cross straight away. The journey across the gate bridge takes us 10 minutes, which means that we will arrive on the other side at 12:45hrs.

We now have to make the final journey along the B120 towards the hospital.

The distance is 40 miles in total and we can travel at a maximum speed of 40 miles per hour. In order to calculate the time we need to use the following calculation:

Time = Distance / Speed Time = 40 / 40
Answer = 1 hour

ANSWER: Arrive at the hospital at 13:45hrs.

Question 3
Based on the sailor arriving at Flitterby at the latest time possible, what time will you reach the Hospital if you choose route 3?

The sailor arrives at Flitterby at 10:45hrs. It takes 5 minutes to load him into the ambulance which brings the time to 10:50hrs. It takes 10 minutes to get to the A11 junction which brings the time to 11:00hrs.

Travelling along route 3 we know that we can achieve a maximum speed of 70 miles per hour. In order to work out the total time it will take us to reach the hospital we need to use the following calculation:

Time = Distance / Speed Time = 280 / 70
Answer = 4 hours

ANSWER: Arrive at the hospital will be 15:00hrs.

Question 4
Based on the sailor arriving at Flitterby at the latest time possible, what time will you reach the Hospital if you choose route 1?

The sailor arrives at Flitterby at 10:45hrs. It takes 5 minutes to load him into the ambulance which brings the time to 10:50hrs. It takes 10 minutes to get to the A11 junction which brings the time to 11:00hrs.

Travelling route 1, it is a total of 80 miles to the Gate Bridge. We are able to travel at a maximum speed of 40mph. To find out the time it takes to travel this distance we need to use the following calculation:

Time = Distance / Speed Time = 80 / 40
Answer = 2 hours

We now know that we will arrive at the Gate Bridge at 13:00hrs. From the information provided we know that the Gate Bridge is open 3 times per hour for 12 minutes. The bridge is open at 10 minutes past, 30 minutes past and 10 minutes to the hour.

The bridge is still open when we arrive at 13:00 hours; therefore we are able to cross straight away. The journey across the gate bridge takes us 10 minutes, which means that we will arrive on the other side at 13:10hrs.

We now have to make the final journey along the B120 towards the hospital.

The distance is 40 miles in total and we can travel at a maximum speed of 40 miles per hour. In order to calculate the time we need to use the following calculation:

Time = Distance / Speed Time = 40 / 40
Answer = 1 hour

ANSWER: Arrive at the hospital at 14:10hrs.

Question 5
Based on the sailor arriving at Flitterby at the earliest time possible, what time will you reach the Hospital if you choose route 2?

The sailor arrives at Flitterby at 10:20hrs. It takes 5 minutes to load him into the ambulance which brings the time to 10:25hrs. It takes 10 minutes to get to the A11 junction which brings the time to 10:35hrs.

We know that the distance from the A11 junction to the edge of the congestion zone is a total of 90 miles. We also know that the distance from the other side of the congestion zone to the hospital along the A424 is a total of 70 miles. Therefore we can add these two distances together to get a total distance (minus the congestion zone area) of 160 miles. In order to work out the time it takes to travel this distance we need to use the following calculation:

Time = Distance / Speed Time = 160 / 40
Answer = 4 hours

We now need to work out the time it will take us to travel through the congestion zone. We know from the map that the distance inside the congestion zone is a total of 10 miles. We can only travel at a maximum speed of 5mph; therefore the calculation used to find out the total time it takes to travel through the congestion zone is as follows:

Time = Distance / Speed Time = 10 / 5
Answer = 2 hours

All we need to do now is add the two travelling times together to reach a total of 6 hours travelling time.

ANSWER: Arrive at the hospital at 16:35hrs

MORE SPEED, DISTANCE AND TIME QUESTIONS

There are 100 questions. You have 20 minutes to answer as many as possible. You are not permitted to use a calculator or write down your calculations. Work out the questions in your head.

Q1. At 4 mph, how long does it take to travel 1 miles?	
Q2. At 120 mph, how long does it take to travel 60 miles?	
Q3. At 30 mph, how far do you travel in 1 hour and 36 mins?	
Q4. At 1 mph, how long does it take to travel 15 miles?	
Q5. At 13 mph, how long does it take to travel 13 miles?	
Q6. At 3 mph, how long does it take to travel 13 miles?	
Q7. At 19 mph, how long does it take to travel 19 miles?	
Q8. At 3 mph, how long does it take to travel 11 miles?	
Q9. At 60 mph, how far do you travel in 1 hour?	
Q10. At 36 mph, how far do you travel in 15 mins?	
Q11. At 15 mph, how long does it take to travel 40 miles?	
Q12. What speed covers 90 miles in 2 hours?	
Q13. At 165 mph, how long does it take to travel 132 miles?	
Q14. At 9 mph, how long does it take to travel 18 miles?	
Q15. What speed covers 20 miles in 2 hours?	

Q16. At 15 mph, how long does it take to travel 88 miles?	
Q17. At 16 mph, how far do you travel in 3 hours?	
Q18. At 72 mph, how far do you travel in 25 mins?	
Q19. At 38 mph, how long does it take to travel 57 miles?	
Q20. What speed covers 19 miles in 1 hour?	
Q21. At 156 mph, how far do you travel in 1 hour?	
Q22. At 200 mph, how long does it take to travel 160 miles?	
Q23. What speed covers 36 miles in 1 hour?	
Q24 What speed covers 15 miles in 15 hours?	
Q25. What speed covers 3 miles in 10 mins?	
Q26. What speed covers 8 miles in 24 mins?	
Q27. At 80 mph, how long does it take to travel 140 miles?	
Q28. At 10 mph, how long does it take to travel 10 miles?	
Q29. At 170 mph, how far do you travel in 1 hour?	
Q30. At 20 mph, how long does it take to travel 7 miles?	
Q31. At 135 mph, how long does it take to travel 72 miles?	
Q32. What speed covers 18 miles in 10 mins?	
Q33. At 16 mph, how long does it take to travel 12 miles?	
Q34. At 2 mph, how long does it take to travel 19 miles?	

Q35. What speed covers 10 miles in 1 hour and 15 mins?	
Q36. At 16 mph, how long does it take to travel 20 miles?	
Q37. At 18 mph, how long does it take to travel 180 miles?	
Q38. What speed covers 80 miles in 4 hours?	
Q39. At 60 mph, how long does it take to travel 120 miles?	
Q40. At 80 mph, how far do you travel in 27 mins?	
Q41. What speed covers 24 miles in 2 hours and 24 mins?	
Q42. At 54 mph, how long does it take to travel 18 miles?	
Q43. What speed covers 48 miles in 15 mins?	
Q44. At 10 mph, how long does it take to travel 12 miles?	
Q45. What speed covers 45 miles in 1 hour and 40 mins?	
Q46. At 100 mph, how far do you travel in 18 mins?	
Q47. What speed covers 2 miles in 20 mins?	
Q48. At 44 mph, how far do you travel in 6 hours and 15 mins?	
Q49. At 5 mph, how long does it take to travel 5 miles?	
Q50. What speed covers 14 miles in 2 hours?	
Q51. What speed covers 15 miles in 2 hours and 30 mins?	
Q52. What speed covers 6 miles in 1 hour and 30 mins?	
Q53. At 2 mph, how long does it take to travel 19 miles?	

Q54. At 20 mph, how far do you travel in 3 hours and 15 mins?	
Q55. At 18 mph, how far do you travel in 20 mins?	
Q56. At 16 mph, how far do you travel in 1 hour and 15 mins?	
Q57. What speed covers 2 miles in 40 mins?	
Q58. What speed covers 8 miles in 1 hour?	
Q59. What speed covers 11 miles in 1 hour?	
Q60. What speed covers 6 miles in 10 mins?	
Q61. What speed covers 25 miles in 10 mins?	
Q62. What speed covers 28 miles in 16 mins?	
Q63. At 10 mph, how far do you travel in 6 mins?	
Q64. What speed covers 14 miles in 1 hour and 24 mins?	
Q65. At 8 mph, how far do you travel in 4 hours?	
Q66. What speed covers 14 miles in 2 hours?	
Q67. At 28 mph, how long does it take to travel 84 miles?	
Q68. At 15 mph, how far do you travel in 1 hour and 20 mins?	
Q69. At 5 mph, how long does it take to travel 16 miles?	
Q70. What speed covers 14 miles in 2 hours?	
Q71. What speed covers 40 miles in 8 hours?	
Q72. At 6 mph, how long does it take to travel 6 miles?	
Q73. At 30 mph, how long does it take to travel 28 miles?	

Q74. What speed covers 15 miles in 3 hours?	
Q75. What speed covers 6 miles in 45 mins?	
Q76. What speed covers 4 miles in 20 mins?	
Q77. At 12 mph, how far do you travel in 2 hours?	
Q78. At 17 mph, how long does it take to travel 17 miles?	
Q79. What speed covers 34 miles in 24 mins?	
Q80. At 36 mph, how long does it take to travel 15 miles?	
Q81. What speed covers 57 miles in 9 hours and 30 mins?	
Q82. At 68 mph, how far do you travel in 1 hour?	
Q83. What speed covers 8 miles in 6 mins?	
Q84. At 19 mph, how long does it take to travel 76 miles?	
Q85. At 117 mph, how far do you travel in 1 hour and 40 mins?	
Q86. At 27 mph, how far do you travel in 1 hour and 20 mins?	
Q87. At 8 mph, how long does it take to travel 8 miles?	
Q88. At 6 mph, how far do you travel in 21 hours and 20 mins?	
Q89. At 7 mph, how far do you travel in 2 hours?	
Q90. What speed covers 84 miles in 36 mins?	
Q91. At 16 mph, how far do you travel in 6 hours and 15 mins?	
Q92. What speed covers 19 miles in 1 hour?	

Q93. At 36 mph, how long does it take to travel 120 miles?	
Q94. What speed covers 13 miles in 1 hour?	
Q95. At 9 mph, how far do you travel in 1 hour and 20 mins?	
Q96. What speed covers 15 miles in 12 mins?	
Q97. What speed covers 11 miles in 15 mins?	
Q98. What speed covers 14 miles in 1 hour and 10 mins?	
Q99. At 44 mph, how long does it take to travel 44 miles?	
Q100. At 105 mph, how long does it take to travel 63 miles?	

ANSWERS TO MORE SPEED, DISTANCE AND TIME QUESTIONS

1. 15 mins	39. 2 hours	77. 24 miles
2. 30 mins	40. 36 miles	78. 1 hour
3. 48 miles	41. 10 mph	79. 85 mph
4. 15 hours	42. 20 mins	80. 25 mins
5. 1 hour	43. 192 mph	81. 6 mph
6. 4 hours & 20 mins	44. 1 hour & 12 mins	82. 68 miles
7. 1 hour	45. 27 mph	83. 80 mph
8. 3 hours & 40 mins	46. 30 miles	84. 4 hours
9. 60 miles	47. 6 mph	85. 195 miles
10. 9 miles	48. 275 miles	86. 36 miles
11. 2 hours & 40 mins	49. 1 hour	87. 1 hour
12. 45 mph	50. 7 mph	88. 128 miles
13. 48 mins	51. 6 mph	89. 14 miles
14. 2 hours	52. 4 mph	90. 140 mph
15. 10 mph	53. 20 mph	91. 100 miles
16. 5 hours & 52 mins	54. 65 miles	92. 19 mph
17. 48 miles	55. 6 miles	93. 3 hours & 20 mins
18. 30 miles	56. 20 miles	94. 13 mph
19. 1 hour & 30 mins	57. 3 mph	95. 12 miles
20. 19 mph	58. 8 mph	96. 75 mph
21. 156 miles	59. 11 mph	97. 44 mph
22. 48 mins	60. 36 mph	98. 12 mph
23. 36 mph	61. 150 mph	99. 1 hour
24. 1 mph	62. 105 mph	100. 36 mins
25. 18 mph	63. 1 mile	
26. 20 mph	64. 10 mph	
27. 1 hour & 45 mins	65. 32 miles	
28. 1 hour	66. 7 mph	
29. 170 miles	67. 3 hours	
30. 21 mins	68. 20 miles	
31. 32 mins	69. 3 hours & 12 mins	
32. 108 mph	70. 7 mph	
33. 45 mins	71. 5 mph	
34. 9 hours & 30 mins	72. 1 hour	
35. 8 mph	73. 56 mins	
36. 1 hour & 15 mins	74. 5 mph	
37. 10 hours	75. 8 mph	
38. 20 mph	76. 12 mph	

Chapter 8
How to Pass the AIB Interview

During this section of the guide I will provide you with a number of sample interview questions and advice on how to answer them. Whilst some of the questions will appear to be easy to answer, it is still important that we cover them, in order to ensure that you are fully prepared for you AIB. I also recommend that you re-visit the AFCO filter interview section of the guide as some of the questions asked may be duplicated.

I have divided the sample questions into various different sections to assist you during your preparation.

SECTION 1 – PERSONAL QUESTIONS
Q. When and where were you born?
Q. Where are you living now and who are you living with?
Q. Where else have you lived apart from with your parents?
Q. Describe your home life to me.
Q. What was your life like growing up?

TIPS:
- Questions that relate to your home life are designed to assess how stable you are as person, whether or not you have any responsibilities at home, whether you are generally a happy person and also what you have learnt from life's experiences to date.
- Know key dates of where you have lived.
- Try and provide examples of where you have moved around. This demonstrates that you are flexible and adaptable when the need arises.
- It is preferable that your home life is stable.
- The more responsibilities you have at home, such as washing, ironing, cleaning, financial responsibilities etc, the better.
- If you have lived with other people, apart from your immediate family, tell them so. Remember – as a Royal Marines Officer you will be living with men and women of different ages etc.

EDUCATION
Q. How many schools have you attended and what years did you attend them?
Q. What did you think about your teachers?
Q. Tell me about your exam results; did you achieve the grades you

wanted?
Q. Could you have worked harder whilst at school?

TIPS:
Although these are relatively easy questions to respond to, ones that relate to your exam results and how hard you worked whilst at school could catch you out. You have to be honest about your results. If they were not up to the standard that you expected, have a valid reason why. Never be disrespectful of your teachers or the educational system. Remember that you are applying to join a disciplined service.

School/college
Q. Did you learn anything from other students?
Q. Did you have any responsibilities whilst at school or college?
Q. What sports did you participate in whilst at school or college?
Q. What clubs or societies were you a member of?
Q. Do you have the Duke of Edinburgh or similar awards?
Q. Where did you travel with school?
Q. Did you have any gaps in your education?

TIPS:
If you did have any gaps in your education, it is better to say that you used the time wisely. Maybe you went travelling around the world in order to gain new experiences and cultures, or maybe you wanted to take time out from your studies to take on a work related role or even a charity role. Whatever you do, do not say that you did nothing with your time off. If you went travelling, what did you gain from the experience?

Whilst at school or college it would be an advantage if you had some level of responsibility. For example, maybe you were a prefect or head of year, or maybe you were the captain of a sports team. You are applying to become an Officer, which effectively means you are going to be a manager and a leader. Having some previous experience of these important roles will be an advantage. If you haven't had any responsibilities in your life to date, how do you know that you'll be a good leader or manager in the Royal Marines?

Outside interests and hobbies
Q. What sports are you currently engaged in?

Q. What sporting achievements have you gained?

Q. Have you been part of any youth organisations such as the Scouts or Guides?

Q. Describe your hobbies and interests.

Q. Are you currently employed either full-time or part-time?

Q. What did you used to do during your school holidays?

Q. Have you ever travelled? If so, where and when did you go and what did you gain from the experience(s)?

Q. What are you future ambitions or plans?

TIPS:

It is imperative that you demonstrate during the interview that you are an active person. If you sit at home all evening on your computer, playing games and surfing the net, then you are probably not the type of person the Royal Marines are looking for. Demonstrate to the interviewer that you are active, a team player and have hobbies and interests that challenge you both mentally and physically.

EMPLOYMENT

Q. What jobs have you had to date?

Q. What responsibilities did you have during each job?

Q. Why did you leave each job?

Q. Did you complete any courses or gain any qualifications during each job?

Q. Who did you have to communicate with in each job?

Q. Were you part of a team or did you work alone?

Q. What were your appraisals like?

TIPS:

If you have no experience in a work-related role to date, how do you know that you will be a good employee for the Royal Marines? Make sure you have some work experience under your belt, even if it's part time work or charity work. Try to also provide examples of responsibilities during each work role and any managerial experience too. These will all work in your favour.

MOTIVATIONAL QUESTIONS

Q. Why do you want to join the Marines? Have you considered the RAF or the Army?

Q. What specifically attracts you to the Royal Marines?
Q. When did you first want to join and has anyone influenced you in your decision to join?
Q. Who have you talked to about a career in the Royal Marines?
Q. How many visits have you had to the Armed Forces Careers Office?
Q. Have you previously attended AIB? If you have, what have you done to improve on last time?
Q. What contact have you had with the Royal Marines? Have you visited any establishments or spoken to any serving members?
Q. Are there any disadvantages for you joining?
Q. What do your family and friends think of you joining?
Q. What branch of the Royal Marines have you applied for?
Q. Would you consider any other branches of the Marines other than the one(s) you have chosen?
Q. What research have you carried out during your preparation for joining the Royal Marines?
Q. Would you consider a Non-Commissioned role if you were unsuccessful at AIB?
Q. What length of commission/service would you like to work?
Q. What qualities are required in order to become a Royal Marines Officer?

TIPS:
Defend your career choice as much as possible. In order to be capable of achieving this, you will need to know it inside out. Make sure you research key information about your chosen branch/career.

KNOWLEDGE OF THE ROYAL NAVY
Q. Tell me what you know about the history of the Royal Navy and the Royal Marines.
Q. What training will you undergo as an Officer?
Q. Do you think you will have any problems or face any challenges during Initial Officer Training?
Q. Tell me what you know about the different aircraft that are used by the Royal Navy and Royal Marines.
Q. Tell me what you know about the different ships that are used by the Royal Navy and the landing craft used by the Marines.
Q. Tell me what you know about the different types of weapons that are carried both on ships, on our aircraft and also used by the Marines.

Q. How would you feel about going to war?

Q. Where are the UK bases of the Royal Marines?

Q. Whereabouts in the world are the Royal Marines operating right now?

CURRENT AFFAIRS QUESTIONS

Current affairs are a very important area of your preparation. You must carry out plenty of research in relation to current affairs. Not only will you need it during the interview(s), but it will also assist you during the essay element of the AIB.

Here are a few important tips to help you research current affairs effectively:

TIP 1: Be careful what paper(s) you read. The type of paper you read will reflect you as a person. If you tell the interviewer that you are an avid reader of The Sun or The Daily Star, you may not be Officer material. In the build up to AIB, try reading The Times, or another quality newspaper.

TIP 2: I would strongly recommend that you subscribe to 'The Week'. This is a fantastic journal that will break down the week's stories for you. This will save having to buy lots of different newspapers.
You can subscribe to the week at the following website:

www.theweek.co.uk

TIP 3: Consider reading The Economist. Once again, this is a quality journal that will provide you with lots of current affairs information.
You can subscribe to the Economist at the following website:

www.economist.com

TIP 4: Don't just research affairs that are relevant to the Royal Marines or the Armed Forces in general. Other topics are just as important!
The purpose of the current affairs section of the AIB interview is designed to assess how informed you are of current global affairs. You should have a general view on each subject and have an understanding

of why the issue is important. Try to have a general view of the whole world with knowledge of a number of issues and events.

Use this format to help you research news and current affairs events:
* What is the subject?
* Why is it significant?
* What is your opinion on it?

SAMPLE CURRENT AFFAIRS QUESTIONS

Q. Take me on a tour of the world and tell me what's caught your eye in the news recently.
Q. Tell me about 6 current affairs from abroad and six from home.
Q. Tell me about a news story from each continent.

USEFUL WEBSITES
BBC News: www.bbc.co.uk/news/

The Times Online: www.timesonline.co.uk

NATO (North Atlantic Treaty Organisation: www.nato.int Ministry of Defence: www.mod.uk

Army: www.army.mod.uk

Royal Navy: www.royalnavy.mod.uk Royal Air Force: www.raf.mod.uk

FINAL INTERVIEW TIPS

* Research key affairs from across the world;
* Have a broad knowledge of current affairs;
* Research affairs that have happened in the last 12 months;
* Focus in detail on events in the last 6 months;
* Select 6 topics for 'home' affairs (e.g. the budget, gang culture);
* Select 6 topics for 'away' affairs. Make sure that you use examples from right across the world;
* Gauge an opinion of each affair (you will need to be able to argue your point);

- Know key facts: people, numbers, locations etc;
- A firm handshake demonstrates a lot about your character;
- Be to the point and concise (don't waffle);
- Hold even eye contact with each boarding officer;
- Avoid hesitations such as "erm, ah, umm" etc;
- Don't use slang;
- Sit up straight and don't slouch;
- Be confident but not overly so!
- Learn the dates and events listed on your application form;
- Make yourself stand out – do something different;
- Be aware of your weaknesses;
- Identify your strengths;
- Think before you speak.

A Few Final Words

You have now reached the end of the guide and no doubt you will be ready to start preparing for the Royal Marines Officer selection process. Just before you go off and start on your preparation, consider the following.

The majority of candidates who pass the selection process have a number of common factors. These are as follows:

1.   They believe in themselves.
The first factor is self-belief. Regardless of what anyone tells you, you can pass the Royal Marines Officer selection process and you can achieve high scores. Just like any job of this nature, you have to be prepared to work hard in order to be successful. The biggest piece of advice I can give you is to concentrate on matching the assessable qualities that form part of the scoring criteria. These would be at the forefront of my mind if I was going through selection right now. Make sure you have the self-belief to pass the selection process and fill your mind with positive thoughts.

2.   They prepare fully.
The second factor is preparation. Those people who achieve in life prepare fully for every eventuality and that is what you must do when you apply to become an Officer with the Royal Marines. Work very hard and concentrate on your weak areas. Within this guide I have spoken a lot about preparation. Identify the areas that you are weak on and go all out to improve them.

3.   They persevere.
Perseverance is a fantastic word. Everybody comes across obstacles or setbacks in their life, but it is what you do about those setbacks that is important. If you fail at something, then ask yourself 'why' you failed. This will allow you to improve for next time and if you keep improving and trying, success will eventually follow. Apply this method of thinking when you apply to join the Royal Marines as an Officer.

4.   They are self-motivated.
How much do you want to join the Royal Marines? Do you want it, or do you *really* want it? When you apply to join you should want it

more than anything in the world. Your levels of self motivation will shine through when you walk into the AFCO and when you attend the Admiralty Interview Board. For the weeks and months leading up to the selection process, be motivated as best you can and always keep your fitness levels up as this will serve to increase your levels of motivation.

Work hard, stay focused, and secure your dream career!

WHY NOT TAKE A LOOK AT OUR ARMED FORCES GUIDES!

FOR MORE INFORMATION ON OUR ARMED FORCES GUIDES, PLEASE CHECK OUT THE FOLLOWING:
WWW.HOW2BECOME.COM

Get Access To
FREE
TEST
QUESTIONS

www.MyPsychometricTests.co.uk

Printed in Great Britain
by Amazon